THE MIRACLE PORTAL

By
Nancy Reynolds

Mastermind Process Steps

1. I believe in a Higher Power, a Mastermind of the universe, who is accessible to me and is interested in helping me achieve my desires.

2. I admit that at a human level I am powerless over my life. I need help to achieve my desires and I ask for that help from the Mastermind, and from my Mastermind partners. I also give my help to them.

3. I've come to believe that a power greater than myself is reminding me of Its universal sanity and order. I believe the activity of the Mastermind is taking place in me right now.

4. I make a decision to place my will and my life under the care and guidance of the Mastermind.

5. I release all anger, resentment, guilt, and blame I've felt toward anyone I've ever known. I release them and let them go. I sincerely ask forgiveness of anyone I may have hurt or offended. I also release myself from all guilt and blame. I forgive.

6. I humbly ask the Mastermind to take complete control of my life and to change **me**, knowing that if I am changed, everything in my life will be different in a corresponding way.

7. I now share my need or desire with my Mastermind group.

8. I express my faith in the power of the Mastermind and I give thanks that it is done. Thank you, Mastermind, it is done! My life is dramatically changed! The Mastermind and I are now partners.

9. I commit myself to hold the vision daily for my Mastermind partners.

COPYRIGHT

Copyright © 2023 by Nancy Reynolds

All rights reserved. No portion of this book may be reproduced in any form without written permission from the publisher or author, except as permitted by U.S. copyright law.

This publication is designed to provide accurate and authoritative information in regard to the subject matter covered. It is sold with the understanding that neither the author nor the publisher is engaged in rendering legal, investment, accounting, or other professional services.

While the publisher and author have used their best efforts in preparing this book, they make no representations or warranties with respect to the accuracy or completeness of the contents of this book and specifically disclaim any implied warranties of merchantability or fitness for a particular purpose. No warranty may be created or extended by sales representatives or written sales materials. The advice and strategies contained herein may not be suitable for your situation. You should consult with a professional when appropriate. Neither the publisher nor the author shall be liable for any loss of profit or any other commercial damages, including but not limited to special, incidental, consequential, personal, or other damages.

Published by P. Hough Bader
Book Cover by KAM.Design

First Edition, 2023
Paperback ISBN: 978-1734382259
eBook ISBN: 979-8223696353
Library of Congress Control Number: 2023916204

THE MIRACLE PORTAL
DEDICATION

This book was born out of a desire to express my gratitude for the help I have received from the Mastermind Process. I hope this book will serve as a guide for other Masterminders.

This book will engage you in new ways of thinking. At the end of the chapters, you will find places to express your new understanding.

Keep this book like a diary, hold it in your confidence. If we had a way to put a lock on it, we would.

Forward

Many wonderful books and podcasts have been released explaining manifestation and the law of attraction. I find it fascinating that over the centuries, and perhaps as long as man has inhabited the earth, this information has been brought forward when it's most needed. Once again, we find ourselves as individuals, a nation, and a world, in a bit of a mess. Again, the Universe gives us just the type of information we need to straighten things out.

This book is written as an addition to what you may have already learned. I have found that, though I intend to hold on to a positive image of what I want and therefore draw it into my life, fear or limited thinking sometimes gets in the way. This is why so many philosophies encourage us to join with like-minded people to receive help in manifesting what we want.

Very simply, I may have trouble believing I can receive my heart's desire. My friend, who is not limited by my self-doubts, may be better able to believe it for me. Our combined thought and support of each other helps us manifest our desires more quickly and easily than either of us could have done alone. This, combined with the always-available help of our Higher Power is the essence of the Mastermind Process.

TABLE OF CONTENTS

Chapter One   1
Meet the Mastermind Process

Chapter Two   9
Mastermind Process Steps

Chapter Three   15
Demonstrations of the Mastermind's Love

Chapter Four   23
Step One

Chapter Five   41
Step Two

Chapter Six   61
Step Three

Chapter Seven   77
Step Four

Chapter Eight   83
Step Five

Chapter Nine   93
Step Six

Chapter Ten   99
Step Seven

Chapter Eleven   109
Step Eight

Chapter Twelve   119
Step Nine

Chapter Thirteen   **123**
   How it's Done.
Chapter Fourteen   **129**
   Forgiveness, Prayer, and The Law of Giving
Chapter Fifteen   **143**
   More Demonstrations

Suggested Authors
Bibliography
Biography

CHAPTER ONE

I've always longed for a process that gives me a sure-fire method for achieving my desires. I found my method in the understanding of a group prayer and growth technique called the Mastermind Process. I believe you can find your miracles here as well.

There is a miracle-working principle in the universe. This principle is always available to help you create miracles in your life. I have seen it proven in my life and in the lives of other Mastermind group members.

You're probably reading this book because you're looking for a miracle, too. And you can have one. Whatever your need or desire, the miracle-working power of Masterminding can bring it into your experience.

The Mastermind Process, or, adherence to a system of applied universal principles, is not new. It is simply reintroduced, through the ages, to those who are ready to believe in it and see their lives permanently altered for the better. The modern-day version of Masterminding began around the turn of the century, in what is called the New Thought movement. Charles Fillmore, the cofounder of the Unity School of Christianity, searched the scriptures to find what he termed, "The Seven Conditions for True Prayer." He recommended these seven conditions to his followers, and great successes manifested. They had physical healings, new financial abundance, and transformations in life circumstances of all kinds.

Then in the 1920s, a Lutheran minister named Frank Buchman had a spiritual experience that caused him to outline a program of self-transformation. Among the tenants of his program was the creation of a support group of like-minded seekers who came to the group for help with relationship issues, physical problems, and financial problems. They sought help to live successful lives. This support group became known as the Oxford group.

They were extremely successful in helping their members. Results began to manifest that were deemed 'miraculous' by observers. Before long the

Oxford group expanded to a worldwide movement. Their healings were numerous and varied and included healings of alcoholism. After a few years, the now sober alcoholics within the movement decided to break away from the Oxford group and formed their own association. This became Alcoholics Anonymous.

Meanwhile, famous industrialists of that era, such as Carnegie, Vanderbilt, and Rockefeller created support groups which they called Mastermind groups. They met weekly and based their financial endeavors on spiritual principles. Their successes were enormous, and Napoleon Hill was so impressed with their achievements he wrote about their methods in his best-selling book, <u>Think and Grow Rich</u>.

Decades later these three powerful concepts were brought together by Jack Boland, a man who knew first-hand the amazing healing powers of a group relying on the Mastermind.

Jack started life with two strikes against him. He was raised by two hopeless alcoholics. He suffered from alcoholism himself. Losing everything important to him, and very nearly losing his life, he joined Alcoholics Anonymous. Jack's life was transformed, and he gave all the credit for this to his Higher Power and the power of the AA group. Eventually, he entered the Unity Ministry program and became one of their most beloved and popular ministers.

When Jack learned about the Seven Conditions for True Prayer described by Unity founder Charles Fillmore, it occurred to Jack that these conditions were not unlike the Twelve Steps he knew from AA. He already knew all about the healing power of group support, and he knew about the Mastermind groups Napoleon Hill described.

Jack also knew from his AA experiences many people were turned off by reference to God or anything religious. He wanted to create a process that touched everyone without demanding any particular religious alliance. He organized the Seven Conditions for True Prayer into a step program. He proposed that these steps be done in group meetings and called the Higher Power of the group the Mastermind.

This was the creation of the Mastermind Process. Jack Boland used his spiritual intuition to create a system of thought, feeling, belief, and group support that could be used by anyone. He popularized Masterminding for his generation.

Jack passed away in 1992, leaving his wonderful lectures on the subject to guide those interested in Masterminding. Sadly, those lectures are now hard to find. Snippets are found on YouTube, under Mastermind, Jack Boland.

At the time of Jack's death, I had been Masterminding for a few years, and was awed and elated by the results my Mastermind partners and I achieved. I felt it was a shame the Mastermind Process was not more widely known. But now, how could it be? There were no books written on the subject. No one was lecturing about Masterminding as Jack had done. How would people hear about his wonderful system of applied spiritual principles?

I decided to try to get the word out myself. I analyzed the process and prepared to write a book about my experiences with Masterminding. I became convinced that there were really nine steps involved, so I expanded a little on Jack's original concept. That created the Mastermind Process I write about today.

This has been the modern-day story of Masterminding. But, long before Jack Boland gave his first lecture on the subject, natural alliances of like-minded people were being formed. Moses, Jesus, Buddha, and all the other great spiritual teachers demonstrated the spiritual principles behind the Mastermind Process. These principles are ancient and eternal. Now you and I are about to explore this same time-honored and proven system of applied spiritual principles.

The Mastermind Process in this book is written for everyone who needs a miracle in their lives and is willing to turn to the Mastermind for help. Despite our seeming differences in approach, all true spiritual seekers have similar experiences and ultimately reach the same end -- demonstrable proof of the Mastermind's love. Let's look at the steps of the Mastermind Process.

What are your expectations for this book?

_____

_____

Nancy Reynolds

_____
_____
_____
_____
_____
_____
_____
_____
_____
_____
_____
_____
_____
_____
_____
_____
_____
_____

Do you have a specific need?

The Miracle Portal

Chapter Two

Mastermind Process Steps

1. I believe in a Higher Power, a Mastermind of the universe, who is accessible to me and is interested in helping me achieve my desires.

2. I admit that at a human level I am powerless over my life. I need help to achieve my desires and I ask for that help from the Mastermind, and from my Mastermind partners. I also give my help to them.

3. I've come to believe that a power greater than myself is reminding me of Its universal sanity and order. I believe the activity of the Mastermind is taking place in me right now.

4. I make a decision to place my will and my life under the care and guidance of the Mastermind.

5. I release all anger, resentment, guilt, and blame I've felt toward anyone I've ever known. I release them and let them go. I sincerely ask forgiveness of anyone I may have hurt or offended.

I also release myself from all guilt and blame. I forgive.

6. I humbly ask the Mastermind to take complete control of my life and to change **me**, knowing that if I am changed, everything in my life will be different in a corresponding way.

7. I now share my need or desire with my Mastermind group.

8. I express my faith in the power of the Mastermind and I give thanks that it is done. Thank you, Mastermind, it is done! My life is dramatically changed! The Mastermind and I are now partners.

9. I commit myself to hold the vision daily for my Mastermind partners.

But that seems so simple, you may say, how could something so simple create miracles?

The Mastermind Process is simple, and living a successful life is simple, but the revolution in thinking required to do so is not always easy. The thoughts and feelings of the world are upside down and backward. That's why dedicated adherence to the steps of the Mastermind Process is needed.

I don't think any of us would suggest the great spiritual leaders of the world walked an easy path. Yet they changed the world by teaching us new ways to think and feel. They centered their thoughts, feelings, and actions on the very best vibration possible -- love.

The worldly mind, which makes up most of our society, doesn't understand it. We are so *un*accustomed to focusing our thoughts and feelings in a positive way we have to create a step process to show us how to do it.

If we are to attain a consistently positive outlook ourselves, we must conform our thoughts, feelings, and actions to the spiritual principles that keep us focused on the positive. The Mastermind Process assists us in this endeavor by providing a clearly outlined path. It is not the only path, but it is an effective one.

Many of you reading this will say something like, "Well Jesus was the Son of God. It was easy for him to focus all his thoughts on love." Yes,

Jesus was the Son of the Mastermind. And so are you. And so am I.

Jesus himself told us that. He corrected those who challenged him by saying, "Is it not written in your law, I said, you are gods!" (John 10:34). We have a responsibility to live up to that title.

When we hear the story of a person who has reached a high level of spiritual attainment, it's tempting to believe they received some sort of special dispensation allowing them to do what we feel we cannot. The struggle of any spiritual master to reach the mountaintop of thought and feeling requires discipline, dedication, and adherence to spiritual principles.

Isn't the Mastermind Process really just another prayer group?

Yes, in one sense a Mastermind group is a prayer group: it allows you to ask for what you want and gives you the support of your Mastermind partners. But it is much more than a prayer group.

The Mastermind Process creates miracles because it is a systematic application of universal spiritual laws.

By believing these principles and using them, you will grow spiritually. You will begin to understand that you, too, are a child of the Mastermind, and you will begin to act like it. You will attract into your life your heart's desires. You and the Mastermind will create miracles!

What are you learning about the way you think and feel?

_____

_____

_____

_____

_____

_____

_____

_____

_____

The Miracle Portal

CHAPTER THREE
Demonstrations of the Mastermind's Love

"And what shall I say further? For time would fail me to tell of Gideon, Barak, Samson, Jephthah, of David and Samuel and the prophets, who by the help of faith subdued kingdoms, administered justice, obtained promised blessings, closed the mouths of lions, extinguished the power of raging fire, escaped the devouring of the sword, out of frailty and weakness won strength and became stalwart, even mighty and resistless in battle." (Hebrews 11:32-35)

The quote above is just one of the Bible's descriptions of what faith and the use of spiritual laws can bring. Can you conceive of anything more impossible, more miraculous, that you need to accomplish in your life than the miracles mentioned above? Do you need to conquer kingdoms of fear and doubt? Do you need justice? Do you need others to honor their commitments? Do you need wild animals of hatred or greed tamed? Do you need the fires of fear and separation quenched? Do you need strength instead of weakness so you can fight with skill the battles in your own life? The Mastermind will meet all your needs, just as it did thousands of years ago. Modern-day Masterminders have their miracles too!

When Mastermind group members talk about receiving their desires, they often refer to the experience as a 'demonstration.' This means they have asked for their desires in their Mastermind group, and the results of their efforts combined with the power of the Mastermind, have resulted in a 'demonstration' of the Mastermind's love. Their desires have been fulfilled.

Through the use of the Mastermind Process miracles have happened in my life and in the lives of other Mastermind group members all over the country.

One of my first demonstrations with the Mastermind group was for employment. Working as a Registered Nurse, I was doing hospital nursing part-time to pay the bills, but I wanted to work with attorneys assisting them with the medical aspects of their cases. I spent the majority of my time trying to build my business. The work wasn't supporting me full-time, and I was tired of the constant struggle. After I began to Mastermind, I took my desire for a steady job working with attorneys to my Mastermind group. The next day I had the idea to ask one of my attorneys to hire me on a full-time basis. I had never discussed such a proposition with him before. Going from working at home and handing in occasional assignments to working full-time in his office would be quite a change. To my amazement, he loved the idea and hired me immediately. I worked happily in that position for several months until a better opportunity came along, at which time I handed my business over to a friend.

Tina, one of my Mastermind partners had the desire to stay at home and work so she could be with her two sons. She was the sole support of their family. Within one week of taking this request to the Mastermind group, she had employment at home which she kept for several months until it was appropriate for her to work outside again. She again took her request for employment to our

Mastermind group and had a position that perfectly fit her specifications within two weeks.

One of the things both Tina and I needed for our work was a computer. We wanted compatible computers because we were working on a project together. The year was 1993, and computers were much more expensive than they are now. Neither Tina nor I had the money (or the credit) with which to purchase a computer. We took our needs to the Mastermind group. Within six weeks we had not one but six computers, four printers, and all the programs we needed to run them. We received all this for $100 on credit because an attorney was getting new computers for his office and was happy to give them away. We used those computers and printers quite successfully for two years until we needed to get new ones. We took the need to the Mastermind again, and within a month or two we were each given the more sophisticated computers and printers that perfectly met our needs.

Carol, another of my Mastermind partners, wanted to go to Egypt for a two-week vacation and seminar. The trip cost $3000, and at the time she had little money. However, she sent in a $150 deposit on faith and then took her desire to the Mastermind group. Money started to come to her from all sorts of unexpected sources. She was asked to teach a parenting class that brought in extra money, and friends and relatives sent birthday presents and Christmas presents of cash instead of gifts. Four months later we were thinking of her fondly as we Masterminded without her, because she was in Egypt!

I've talked with Mastermind group members from two other Mastermind groups in Las Vegas, and also members from groups in San Diego. Here are some of their stories.

Julie from Las Vegas wanted to have a baby. She and her husband tried unsuccessfully for about a year to conceive. They were most discouraged, but when they began Masterminding, they took their desire for a baby to their Mastermind group. Within two months Julie was pregnant and eventually delivered a beautiful, healthy baby girl.

Judy from San Diego owned a maid service. She built up a good clientele but was having trouble getting her clients to pay their bills. She took her need for payment to her Mastermind group, and the next day payments started pouring in. In one day she had collected $1300 in cash, three-quarters of what was owed her.

While she was pumping gas she turned away for a few moments, and her purse, along with the money, was stolen. Judy reported the theft to the police and went home in utter discouragement. She was baffled that the money she had collected through the assistance of the Mastermind could have been stolen from her.

After she was home for a few hours, the doorbell rang, and there stood a policeman with her purse. She accepted the purse with thanks and opened it. All her belongings were there, including the $1300.

Her group leader joked with her, "That money was yours. If you had flushed it down the toilet it would have come out the shower head!"

Alma and Ronnie from San Diego were devoted to Masterminding and had to travel over 100 miles round trip to go to their meeting each week.

The trip down wasn't so much of a problem because they were traveling in daylight, but the return home was difficult because they were traveling in the dark. Their old car had a faulty electrical system. Anytime they traveled more than 30 minutes with the car lights on they blew a fuse. They usually had to pull over four or five times during the trip to change it.

One week, Alma and Ronnie asked in their Mastermind group that their car make it home without breaking down. As they approached their home that night, they realized they hadn't changed a fuse the entire trip back and the lights were still working. They've worked perfectly ever since!

More Mastermind demonstrations are included in the last chapter of this book. Every Mastermind group member I've ever met has said the same thing: once you begin Masterminding, your life is transformed.

I've seen financial needs of all descriptions met repeatedly. I've seen many employment needs filled. I've seen relationship problems of all varieties healed. I've seen healings of pancreatitis, endometriosis, chronic allergies, and arthritis. I've seen long-standing and deep-seated emotional problems healed. I've seen homes and cars and computers and all manner of other material needs met. I've seen people brought together with exactly the right person to assist them in meeting their needs or desires against impossible odds.

I know that the Mastermind will meet the needs of anyone who asks.

Are you encouraged by the success of Mastermind groups?

_____

_____

_____

_____

_____

_____

_____

_____

_____

_____

_____

_____

Chapter Four

Step One

I believe in a Higher Power, a Mastermind of the universe, who is accessible to me and who is interested in helping me achieve my desires.

Do you have a belief in a Higher Power?

Some people call their Higher Power God. Some call It Jesus, or simply Christ, or Buddha, or Confucius, or Moses, or Allah. Some refer to the power of the Universe or the Creator, or the Maker. Some have names for their Higher Power society doesn't recognize. Some refer to their Higher Power as He, some as She, and some as It. Some people have no belief in a Higher Power at all.

In the Mastermind Process you don't need to have a formal belief stemming from a specific religion. If you have strong spiritual beliefs and wish to stay within those beliefs, great! The Mastermind Process will work well for you. If you have no specific beliefs centered around a particular religion, that's also great, the Mastermind Process will work well for you, too!

Do I have to be convinced that a Higher Power exists to use the Mastermind Process?

Yes. Some people, because of prior experiences, or because of their upbringing, are already convinced of the existence of a Higher Power. Others are not so sure. For most people, experience brings conviction.

All that's asked of you in the Mastermind Process is that you be *willing* to suspend your disbelief. If you do that, if you are willing to believe in a Higher Power, the Mastermind will prove to you soon enough that It exists.

Does my Higher Power have to be the same as everyone else's?

No. There are some people who simply cannot acknowledge a 'traditional' Higher Power. In the Twelve Step programs, such people are encouraged to believe in the Higher Power of the group. Your Higher Power can be called anything you like as long as you are willing to believe that a Higher Power *outside yourself* exists.

Doesn't the Mastermind take offense at not being called by Its true name?

The Higher Power who created you and this universe loves you so much! And It's not petty. We could call It by any name we like. You could say 'Mastermind' or 'lawn mower,' and it wouldn't make any difference. Your Higher Power is interested in the quality of your thoughts, and the dedication of your love. It really doesn't matter what name you use, you will still get the same results. What matters is what's in your heart.

In the Mastermind Process, the term Mastermind is used to refer to everyone's Higher Power. This gives everyone in the group a common frame of reference. The name Mastermind also reminds the group the Higher Power working with them is the Mastermind or Intelligence behind the entire universe, It is the original Creator Mind.

Why should I believe that a Higher Power or Mastermind will assist me?

The Miracle Portal

Sometimes people have been so wounded or disappointed in their prior belief systems, they are afraid to risk believing in the assistance of the Mastermind. They may believe that some sort of Higher Power created them and the universe, but they have never seen Its assistance work personally for them.

There is a belief rampant in the world, suggesting we are poor, powerless, sinful mortals who don't deserve the Mastermind's help. That is absolutely untrue.

We are the children of the Mastermind! It's interested in helping us because It is our Creator. We are Its children.

The Mastermind is eager to help us. Jesus came here to demonstrate how directly tied to the Mastermind are Its children. The problem is, we have forgotten that.

Some people even became so discouraged that one major magazine asked the question, 'Is God dead?' The answer is, 'No!' The Mastermind who created you and this universe is as alive and active today as It ever was. All that's necessary for you to prove Its existence and interest in you is that you be willing to believe, even if you're afraid. If you're willing to believe, the Mastermind will do the rest.

I have a favorite little story about how the Mastermind demonstrated Its existence to Tina, one of my Mastermind partners. This happened years before we formed our Mastermind group.

It was during the time when Tina was in a good deal of spiritual turmoil. She was pregnant, and she offered the Mastermind this challenge: "If You really exist, show me! Make this baby red-haired and blue-eyed." Tina is dark-haired and dark-eyed. She comes from a family of seven children, and none of them, nor her parents have red hair or blue eyes. Her husband was dark-haired and brown-eyed like the rest of his family. Yet when Tina's son was born, he was red-haired and blue-eyed just as he is today! It was a cute little miracle, and you can believe me when I tell you that Tina never again doubted the existence of the Mastermind!

Stories such as these are fun and interesting but they have no real meaning to you until you test the Mastermind yourself. The only way you will ever know if this process works is to try it! Of course, I always love it when people begin Masterminding because I get to hear all the wonderful stories of their personal miracles!

What are the attributes or qualities of the Mastermind?

The Mastermind is present everywhere and at all times. It is all-knowing, all-wise, all-powerful good. It is universal Mind. It is the universal principle, the ideal of love and goodness. It is the Creator and Maintainer of all life. It is the ultimate Truth. It is Spirit – thought. Thought is the true substance of all things, and Its spiritual substance is individualized in us as Soul.

We have within us the spark of the Mastermind. It is all the power in the universe. It is also personally interested in you.

Why should the Mastermind, who includes all these marvelous attributes and qualities be interested in me?

Because you are Its creation. You are the child of the Mastermind. I say that so often because it's very difficult for most of us to hear.

Many of the world's religions imply that there is or will be only one Son of the Mastermind. But Jesus, the man who many regard as the 'only' Son of the Mastermind, didn't say that. Over and over in the scriptures, he speaks to his followers about their Father the Mastermind. Jesus said, "*I am the way*," not "*I am the one*." "I am the way. Follow me." (John 14:6).

If we are to follow him and become *like* him, then we must believe what he said; not what others said about him.

In the Lord's prayer Jesus begins with the words, '*Our* Father,' not 'My Father.' In the most famous and most often used prayer of all time, Jesus told us clearly that we are all the Mastermind's children. (Matthew 6:9). He told us, "I go unto my Father and *your* Father." (John 14:12).

The Mastermind is interested in you because It is your Creator. And like any other parent, your universal, spiritual parent wants for you all the good things you could want for yourself, and even more.

The Miracle Portal

The Mastermind is interested in you because, as Its child, you also include all Its wonderful and exciting attributes and qualities. You are a Creator. Here you are in the Middle School of Earth learning how to create the life conditions you want, individually and collectively.

You may not be very good at it yet. You may have turned your back upon spiritual principles and done some things you think are pretty *un*spiritual. Even though you may be in the childhood of expressing who you really are, the truth is you will someday fulfill your destiny.

An apple seed will one day be an apple tree. A puppy will one day be a dog. You will one day demonstrate all the qualities of the Mastermind. That is a spiritual principle. An apple seed does not grow into a pear tree, a puppy does not grow up to be a rhinoceros, and you, no matter how it may appear at the moment, cannot 'grow up' to be a struggling mortal.

I'm not saying that you're going to achieve perfection in this one lifetime. There are all sorts of beliefs about what happens after we leave this world. By whatever divine process, in this world or the next, in this lifetime or the next; You, I, the neighbor you hate, the neighbor you love, all of us will one day achieve perfection.

You were created to become the perfect expression of all-powerful love, and that is exactly what, one day, you will become. How could anyone, including the Mastermind, not be interested in such a magnificent being?

Okay, the Mastermind may be interested in me. But how is It accessible to me?

Through thought and feeling. Our thoughts and feelings create our experiences both individually and collectively. Thought is spirit. Thought is energy. It is the basic building block of the universe.

We mold our world with our thoughts and feelings about it, and we mold our personalities with our thoughts and feelings about ourselves. Proverbs 23:7 says, "As a man thinketh in his heart, so is he."

There is no more powerful medium of communication in the universe than thought and feeling. Doesn't it make sense then, that the

The Miracle Portal

Creator of the universe would use thought to make Itself accessible to us?

When the Mastermind works with us to meet our heart's desires, It does so by responding to our thoughts and feelings. And when we hinder our own desires by getting on the wrong track with our thoughts and feelings, It sends us teachers to get us back on track.

Since thoughts and feelings are so important, let's look at them more closely. In the natural sciences, mathematicians and quantum physicists are beginning to prove that what really makes up our world is our thoughts and feelings -- energy.

They've proven our thoughts and feelings actually change the physical manifestation of the objects around us, starting at the subatomic level.

Just a quick refresher of physics will remind you that things of the world are made-up of matter, which breaks down to molecules, which break down to atomic particles, which break down to subatomic particles.

We have wonderful names for subatomic particles like 'quarks,' 'charms,' and 'neutrinos.' These particles are so tiny they're actually more theory than physical particles. We can't see them, even with an electron microscope. In fact, the only way the scientists who study them can prove they exist is by photographing their trails as they're shot through slabs of lead.

Scientists have found that each type of subatomic particle has its own 'signature' trail. Interestingly, scientists studying the subatomic trails found there was no difference in their substance. The differences were in their *rate of vibration*. They also found the particles changed vibration (and therefore signature trails) depending upon what the scientist wanted or expected.

So if the scientist wanted the particle to leave a quark signature trail it would. And if he wanted it to leave a charm trail, it would, or a neutrino trail, it would.

The subatomic particles responded to the scientist's thoughts and feelings. Expanding on these findings we can extrapolate this: our thoughts and feelings create an energy *vibration*. This energy vibration in the physical world creates subatomic particles. These subatomic particles create atomic particles, which clump together to form atoms, which form molecules, which form matter. Even science can now theorize that our thoughts and feelings create our reality.

This is why no two people see the world in exactly the same way. Each person's worldview is slightly different, because each person's world is literally different, depending on their thoughts and feelings about it, starting at a subatomic level.

It doesn't stop there. We said earlier that our thoughts and feelings create our worlds individually and collectively. When we look at collective thought, we must understand that the thoughts and feelings of everyone who now lives, or has ever lived on planet earth, form what the famous psychiatrist Carl Yung called the 'collective unconscious.'

The thoughts and feelings of this collective unconscious influence all of us constantly. Thoughts do not have to be verbalized to have influence. All beings can communicate telepathically though we may not be aware of that ability on the conscious level.

Over eons of time, our collective thoughts and feelings have created what might be called 'thought forms.' These thought forms are the basis of our collective reality. They have become our agreed-upon rules of the game for planet Earth. Some rules are pleasant, but some of them are unpleasant.

Jesus tried to confront and disrupt our beliefs and fears about some of these collective thought forms. We've been awfully slow to get the idea.

He told us to love when the world said to hate. He told us to believe in life when the world said to believe in death. He told us to believe in health when the world said to believe in sickness. He told us to believe in abundance when the world said to believe in scarcity.

The trouble is most people didn't believe him. Most of the people now, still don't believe him.

When he left the physical plane, after proving death had no dominion over him, he told us the Mastermind would send us a 'Comforter.' We call this Comforter the Holy Spirit (John 14:26). It is constantly with us to remind us of the things Jesus taught.

The Holy Spirit is also sometimes referred to as the "still small voice." It is the voice of inner knowing. It often flies in the face of conventional wisdom.

I grant you that sometimes, with the daily deafening racket of world thought, it's hard to hear your inner voice, which is your sure guidance out of any predicament. It's hard to pay attention to its instructions when we've asked for help. It may take some practice, commitment, and concentration. But you will learn that because you asked for assistance the Mastermind will find a way to communicate with you.

Okay. I'm willing to believe there is a Higher Power we'll call the Mastermind. And I'm willing to let the Mastermind contact me through my thoughts and feelings. And I'm even willing to believe that because the Mastermind created me, It's interested in me. But I'm kind of stuck on this thing about It being interested enough to help me achieve my desires. Why should the Mastermind of the universe care if I get what I want?

Have you ever noticed that people around you desire an endless variety of different things? Where did these diverse desires come from?

We all desire security: a safe place to live, food to eat, clothes to wear, and people to love us. But over and above these basics, we are individuals in deciding what other 'perks' we want.

Could there possibly be a plan, a universal reason behind our multitude of desires? Yes. We are the children of the Mastermind. We come to the physical world to learn and grow, and our desires help lead us onward towards our growth and the growth of those around us.

Dr. H. Emilie Cady, in her wonderful book, <u>Lessons in Truth</u>, writes: "The only way God has of letting us know of His infinite supply and His desire to make it ours is for Him to push gently on the divine spark living within each one of us. He wants you to be a strong, self-sufficient man or woman, to have more power and dominion over all before you; so He quietly and silently pushes a little more of Himself, His desire, into the center of your being. He enlarges, so to speak, your real self, and at once you become conscious of a new desire to be bigger, calmer, grander, stronger. If He had not pushed it in the center of your being first, you would never have thought of new desires, but would have remained perfectly content as you were."

You may not know how your desire benefits you and the world, but it does. We are all so interconnected that what benefits one benefits all of us.

In fact, because the Mastermind expresses through us, our true desires are really Its desires. Doctor Cady goes on to say, "Someone asked: 'Suppose I desire my neighbor's wife or his property; is that desire born of God?' You do not and cannot by any possibility, desire that which belongs to another. You do not desire your neighbor's wife. You desire the love that seems to you to be represented by your neighbor's wife... You do not in reality desire anything that belongs to your neighbor. You want the equivalent of that for which his possessions stand. You want your own."

The Mastermind looks at our desires with delight and anticipation, anxious to see how they will lead us to grow. It's true that sometimes we lose sight of our relationship with the Mastermind and try to achieve our desires in negative ways. We learn from these mistakes too, though they may be deeply painful lessons.

As you go along in your own personal experience of Masterminding, I believe you'll understand the multiple blessings that accompany your desires more and more. But for now, let's just agree that your desires mean more than you think, and the Mastermind uses them to benefit everyone.

There is a Higher Power, a Mastermind of the universe, who is accessible to you through your thoughts and feelings. The Mastermind Creator is interested in you personally. You are Its child. It loves you and wants to help you achieve your true desires because your desires are also Its desires.

How different is the Mastermind from your previous religious beliefs?

_____

_____

_____

The Miracle Portal

CHAPTER FIVE

Step Two

I admit that at a human level, I am powerless over my life. I need help to achieve my desires. I ask for that help from the Mastermind, and from my Mastermind partners. I also give my help to them.

What is the human level of existence?

Have you noticed the world does not exactly resemble your idea of heaven? Yet spiritual teachers from all faiths have told us heaven exists here and now. Jesus said, "The Kingdom of Heaven is within you." (Luke 17:21).

It doesn't seem that way to you? If heaven is within you, you certainly haven't seen it? That's because you're judging your world from the human level, with your human mind, which doesn't see things accurately.

You judge from the human level when you judge exclusively by the five physical senses. You judge from the human level when you have to 'see it to believe it.' You judge from the human level when you rely on your experiences of the past to predict your future. You judge from the human level when you rely on the human beliefs of others to guide you. You judge from the human level when you exclude the Mastermind.

The human level of beliefs and opinions has been known by a variety of names. Some have called it the human mind. Some call it mortal mind. Some call it the ego. In the Bible, Paul called it the carnal mind.

Actually, it's that 'little' mind of yours that believes it's separate from the Mastermind. The ego mind believes it can think for itself and plan things out on its own. It believes its way is the best.

There is no mind separate from the Mastermind. Our experiences in this world seem to contradict this. The challenge of this world is to look beyond the binary -- good and evil, young and old, short and tall, etc.

We believe in a lot of separate and competing minds, and limited resources. These are ideas of the human mind.

In the channeled work, A Course in Miracles, by Dr. Helen Schucman-Scribe, the first paragraph says, "Nothing real can be threatened. Nothing unreal exists. Herein lies the peace of God."

This statement is profound. It's saying, *'Everything real is eternal* and may change form, but cannot be threatened with oblivion. *Everything unreal may exist for a time, but is not eternal.'*

Can you see how many situations on the human level are *unreal* in the sense that they are not eternal? Our bodies are not eternal nor is any physical thing in existence. All of it seems very real. However, if we use the strictest criteria to judge, we can see the physical world is not real in the sense that it is not eternal.

What *is* eternal? Spirit, thought, and energy is eternal. The *idea* behind every physical creation is eternal. The *soul* energy behind every person and every creature is eternal. The rest is temporary, used for a time on the material plane where we come to learn.

I can share a personal experience of this truth with you. I once had to choose to believe in the

Mastermind's creation of a world of love or die trying.

Several years ago I stopped by my office complex on a Saturday evening to pull the chart of a patient involved in an emergency. When I emerged from the office I found my tire was flat. A friendly security guard offered to help me change it.

What I didn't know was this stranger was only posing as a security guard. He had punctured my tire so he could offer to help me change it.

He eeded to go into the building first, he explained, so he could call his watch buddy and tell him he was going off rounds. I let him into the building. As soon as we were alone inside he put a knife to my throat and threatened to kill me if I didn't do as he said.

He tied me up with my belt, cut off my clothes, and raped me. He left me isolated and absolutely helpless while he roamed through the offices looking for money.

As traumatic as the rape was, the thought of dying a violent death was even worse. All sorts of fearful thoughts went through my mind. It was the weekend. If he slit my throat and left me there to die, no one would even find me until Monday, long after I had bled to death.

In the midst of my fear, I began to declare the *truth*. I declared that this man was my brother. He was a child of the Mastermind just as I was, no matter how he seemed to behave. Therefore he could not hurt me. The Mastermind never created one of Its children capable of hurting another. The Mastermind never created another mind who could think up such evil. *The Mastermind's creation is entirely good and therefore this man is entirely good.*

I ran these ideas over and over in my mind regardless of what the attacker did or said. In the end, he said, "Don't get until you count to 100." In the end, I was alive and unhurt.

Moreover, because of that experience, I became the co-founder of the Rape Crisis Intervention center in the town where I lived. Along with other dedicated volunteers, I succeeded in helping many other people who had experienced the same frightening event. Because of our work that town had one of the most responsive and advanced victim assistance programs in the country. This included support from area police, the District Attorney's Office, hospitals, and even the State Legislature.

Would this man have stabbed or killed me if I had not consciously known the truth about him? I don't know. I can only tell you the police felt he'd been stalking me and that I was extremely lucky to have come out of the ordeal as physically unharmed as I did.

I can't tell you I didn't suffer some of the difficult after-effects that many victims of violent crime also suffer – nightmares, phobias, and depression. I had my share of those problems to work through. I can tell you this, something divine happened to me. Because of the hours, I spent declaring the truth about him, I have not had to deal with the anger and hatred toward my attacker that many victims experience.

I certainly don't want a person who commits such acts out on the street. If the police had found him I would have testified against him. But I have never hated my attacker.

Did knowing the truth about him and the situation change the outcome from tragedy to triumph? There's no way I can prove it did. But I believe it did.

The idea that we live surrounded by good is a simple concept, but because of the illusions we live with every day it's often difficult to grasp. So don't struggle with it. Struggle only makes things harder to understand.

Admit to yourself that you don't as yet understand this concept totally (if that's the case) and allow yourself to play with the concept as you continue learning about the Mastermind process.

Wait a minute, aren't you missing some important doctrines here? What about the ideas of the devil and hell?

These are beliefs common to many of the world's religions. Lucifer, one of the Archangels, was supposed to have been so jealous that God was making a human His son, that Lucifer started a war in heaven. In the end, Lucifer and fifteen percent of the angels were permanently cast into hell.

Since then Lucifer, or the devil, or Satan, whatever you wish to call him, has supposedly been waging a war for human souls with the aid of his demons. What a silly and gruesome story!

Many people believe that story is found in the Bible, but that's not true. It seems this story really got its start in John Milton's "Paradise Lost," which is a poem, a work of fiction, written in 1667.

The devil, or Satan, and the whole idea of hell is nothing more than a creation of the human mind. The inventor is *fear*, making us believe we are separate from the Mastermind.

Jesus said, "The Kingdom of Heaven is not here, nor there, but the Kingdom of Heaven is within you." (Luke 17:21). The Kingdom of Heaven is a state of mind, *thought and feeling*. In this state of mind, we are conscious of our oneness with the Mastermind.

It only makes sense that if the Kingdom of Heaven is within us as a state of thought and feeling, so is the realm of hell.

What is the realm of hell? Is it a fiery pit? No. It is a *state of mind* in which we believe we are separated from the Mastermind. Are there people walking around today who are living in hell? You bet! The more we believe in separation between ourselves and the all-loving Mastermind, the more we believe we live in hell.

Does that make hell the creation of the Mastermind? No! Does it mean we're doomed to stay forever in that state of thought and feeling? Again, no.

The moment we stop believing we have ever been separated from the Mastermind, we stop living in hell. We created hell, the Mastermind did not.

Likewise, is there really a fallen angel tempting us to do wrong? No. But we do sometimes listen to our own human minds when they suggest we should perceive or act without love.

When we do that, we can act like devils. The ancients probably came closest to the truth when they spoke of every child being born with an angel on one shoulder and a devil on the other. These aren't really angelic or demonic entities. They're the divine and human aspects of ourselves. We choose who we listen to. We can respond to the human or we can respond to the divine.

Devilish thought is about human self-interest, usually guarding against fear. This thinking opposes the Mastermind and the principles of Love. This is what leads to earthly evils and is the true devil.

But wait a minute. Jesus talked about hell and the devil.

Yes, he did. Let's inspect what he said. One familiar reference is in the Sermon on the Mount. Jesus talked about speaking badly of other people, and he said, "Whosoever says you cursed fool! [You empty-headed idiot], shall be liable to and unable to escape the hell (Gehenna) of fire. (Matthew 5:22).

In Palestine, there was a town dump called the Valley of Hinnom or Gehenna. It was a terrible place where people put dead animal carcasses, and the bodies of dead criminals, as well as all manner of trash. Just like in today's trash dumps, the fermentation of the trash caused fires. There was always a fire simmering under the heaps of trash. Jesus was literally saying whoever speaks ill of another will wind up on the burning trash heap. The Law of Attraction. He was not referring to a destination after death in which there was eternal torment.

Let's look at the devil and demons. We've heard the story of the woman with the issue of blood, or the boy with seizures, or the madman of Gerasenes possessed of demons. These people were referred to as being tormented by a devil.

We have to look at the context in which this was discussed. In those ancient days in Palestine, people had no knowledge of medical conditions. They believed everyone who had an illness, including persistent vaginal bleeding, epilepsy, or schizophrenia was being tormented by a devil.

I suppose Jesus could have looked at the boy who suffered from epilepsy and told the crowd, "This boy is suffering from a condition in his brain. It periodically has a kind of electrical storm, making him unconscious and making his body jerk. I'm going to heal this condition." He could have said that but no one would have known what in the world he was talking about. So he spoke in concepts the people could understand. He "cast out devils." Today we would say, "He healed illnesses."

Jesus always spoke in ways the average person could understand. He spoke of shepherds and sheep, he spoke of grapes and vines, he spoke of trash heaps and he spoke of devils of illness.

Some evil being is not following us around contrary to the will and might of the Mastermind, causing us torment.

Well, maybe so but I've heard that the devil has the power to assume a pleasing form. What if you're just being deceived?

If there's any deceit by a 'devil,' it's in our ability to make ourselves believe a fiction born of our imaginations. We accept the idea of a devil because we run from the responsibility of living by spiritual principles. It's much less painful to believe 'the devil made me do it,' than to admit to ourselves we made a mistake and we're responsible for correcting it.

What is the other implication? A being who is inherently evil could assume the powers of all good and thereby deceive us? There is no power greater than the Mastermind, so this is obviously nonsense. There is no devil except the one we create ourselves by listening to our lower aspect and then acting upon it.

We abdicate all personal responsibility when we ascribe such temptations to a demonic force and not to our carnal minds. There is no evil except that which we create ourselves by believing there is a power apart from the Mastermind.

There is no hell except that which we create ourselves by believing we are separate from the Mastermind. "God hath made man upright but man hath sought out many inventions." (Ecclesiastes 7:29).

Why does looking at the world and living my life from the human level make me powerless over my life?

You are powerless over your life because when living life from the human level you do not see reality. The Mastermind created a universe in which all are united with It forever, and all creation is constantly supplied and blessed by Its love. The moment you identify a desire the Mastermind agrees with it and sends it to you.

Everyone and everything you see was created as a spiritual idea meant to express the essence of the Mastermind -- love. The only way to block the Mastermind's constant supply of good is to turn our backs and refuse to receive.

The human mind creates a reality based on fear and separation. In our ignorance, we believe this lie and turn our backs on the Mastermind. We turn our backs on our own good.

The judgment and actions you make from a human level are based upon protecting yourself from loss and pain. The more you believe in fear and separation, the further you will travel from the truth of your oneness with the Mastermind. The more you believe in separation from the Mastermind and each other, the more lost and miserable you will become.

Living at the human level you will look for human solutions to your problems and will seek input from others who are making erroneous judgments based on their beliefs in separation from the Mastermind.

In your pain and confusion, you will forget that you are telepathically in touch with every other human mind on the planet and you will let this collective version of reality influence your thinking.

Finally, you will sink into despair fed by a belief in separation, fear, guilt, conflict, evil, and death.

Then a remarkable thing may happen. In your despair, you may realize **there must be a better way.** You may reach out to a power greater than yourself. The Mastermind gave us free will and it is only when we consciously turn to It for help that the Mastermind **can** help us. You **must** ask for help.

Is that why I need help to achieve my desires?

Yes. The moment you have a desire the Mastermind begins to arrange the universe to meet it. Every desire has its own vibratory level. You must raise the level of your thoughts and feelings to vibrate at a level matching your desire. In that way, you bring your desire out of the invisible and into your experience.

The trouble is, it's sometimes hard to believe something that good is on its way to us. We are frightened by experiences of the past or world belief and we are plagued with self-doubts. Our human minds give us a running commentary of all the reasons we can't have it.

Sometimes we're even afraid to ask for what we want because we didn't get what we wanted from Mom and Dad and we project onto the Mastermind the fears we had about our human parents.

It is often easier for our friends to believe good things for us than it is for us to believe them for ourselves. Our Mastermind partners are not hindered by our fears and erroneous beliefs. Isn't it easier for you to believe that your friend deserves his heart's desire than to believe it for yourself?

Mastermind partners help each other see through the illusions of the human mind. We remind each other of spiritual principles. We affirm together that we are entirely safe in the Mastermind's love. Together we give thanks that all our needs are met. Your friend's encouragement can help raise your vibrational level to the point where your desire becomes manifest.

Jesus said, "I tell you that if two of you on earth agree about anything you ask for, it will be done for you by my Father in heaven. For where two or three come together in my name [or my vibrational level] there am I with them." (Matthew 18:19 and 20).

Jesus's level of vibration was extremely high, maybe the highest ever known on Earth. In this quote, Jesus tells us whenever two or more people come together in high vibrations to work on their problems using spiritual principles, the Mastermind will be there with them.

Some of the greatest spiritual leaders of the ages formed Mastermind groups. They didn't call them 'Mastermind groups,' but they were still groups of like-minded people who were consciously working on their problems using spiritual principles.

Moses had a Mastermind group with Aaron and Miriam. Jesus, when he was getting ready to go into the world and preach formed a Mastermind group. We call them the Twelve Disciples. Before the crucifixion and resurrection, he formed a *super* Mastermind group (popularly called the

Transfiguration) consisting of Moses and Elijah, and himself. (Matthew 17:1-4). Paul was part of the Mastermind group called the Apostles. The founding fathers of the United States of America were a Mastermind group. Andrew Carnegie and other great industrialists of his time were involved in formal Mastermind groups. All the Twelve Step programs are meant to be Mastermind groups. Throughout the ages, people have recognized the power of a group. Let us start using that power on our own behalf.

It is another spiritual principle that to heal it, one must see through a physical plane illusion and understand the truth about the situation. The illusion will disappear and the perfection the Mastermind created will appear instead. *This is the basis of miracles.* We live in a perfect finished universe. Every desire you ever had is already met. It may not appear that way at the moment but sometimes you have to believe it before you can see it.

This is how your Mastermind partners work for you as well as how you work for them. They know the truth about your desire, for you. They know that because you asked for it, the Mastermind is already providing your desire. As they help you to see that, your vibration of thought and feeling begins to match the vibration of your desire. That pulls it into your experience.

If you would like to achieve your desires with ease and joy, without struggle and pain, I invite you to begin by recognizing when you operate at a human level you are powerless over your life.

Because you are often deceived by illusions, you need help to achieve your desires. Humbly ask the Mastermind, who loves you, to help you achieve these desires.

When a like-minded group works toward the same cause, the vibrational energy is high. Your Mastermind partners can believe for you what you cannot believe for yourself. You need to ask them for help.

Can you describe the human level of existence?

_____
_____
_____

The Miracle Portal

Was there a time in your life when understanding the difference between the spiritual plane and the physical plane would have helped you?

Chapter Six

Step Three

I've come to believe a power greater than myself is reminding me of Its universal sanity and order. I believe the activity of the Mastermind is taking place in me right now.

What is the Mastermind's universal sanity and order?

The Mastermind created a universe that is different in many ways from the one we see with our five physical senses.

When we look at the world from a physical point of view we see duality. We may see either good or bad. When the Mastermind looks at the world, It sees only good because It never created 'bad.'

When we look at the world using our individual human minds, we may see either lack or abundance. The Mastermind sees only abundance.

The Miracle Portal

It never created lack, therefore lack is a physical illusion.

When we look at the world through unenlightened eyes we may see love or fear. When the Mastermind looks at the world It sees only love. It never created fear therefore fear does not really exist. There is no duality in the Mastermind's universe. There is only good.

Let's look at some ways in which we are deceived:

Good/Bad
Rich/Poor
Healthy/Sick
Love/Hate
Faith/Fear
Loved/Abused
Respected/Degraded
Beautiful/Ugly
Abundance/Lack
Peaceful/Troubled

Everything on the left-hand side of this list is truth and is of the Mastermind's creation. Everything on the right side of the list was never created by the Mastermind or anyone but ourselves. It is nothing but human opinion.

I could keep on comparing the unreal human universe with the Mastermind's real and perfect universe, but I think you get the point.

Because we were created in the image and likeness of the Mastermind we are also given the power to create on the physical plane. Since most of us believe in evil we have created things on the human level that look pretty evil. But thankfully, just as we as human parents don't give our children real guns and bombs to play with, the Mastermind doesn't give us 'reality' to play with.

It gives us illusions to play with which look and feel very real. At the end of playtime, it is the Mastermind's version of reality that wins out and is eternal.

As Jesus demonstrated again and again, our illusions cannot stand against the Mastermind's truth. Either here, by recognizing real from illusion on the physical plane, or after death on the spiritual plane, we will find the Mastermind was running things perfectly all along.

Oh great! I'm really living in good even when I see bad, is that it?
Yes.

Then why can't I prove that?
You can. That's part of what Masterminding is all about. All that's needed to see through and undo one of humanity's illusions is to understand that *it is an illusion*. Physical healings are accomplished in this way and material conditions are changed in this way as well.

Let me give you another example of how seeing through the illusions of the world can change material conditions. One of my first experiences in Masterminding occurred several years ago. I was a nurse and had been working in alcohol and chemical dependency treatment. I wanted to move to a little town in northern Arizona so I applied for a position as the director of nursing in a freestanding alcohol and drug treatment facility. After several weeks I reached an agreement with the large corporation that owned the treatment center.

Nancy Reynolds

Everything was set except that a new administrator was taking over the clinic. This was said to be a minor element in our negotiations. The head of corporate personnel approved my hire and felt there would be no problem.

I quit my job and rented a temporary house in the small town where I would be working.

When I arrived, I discovered the new administrator was not at all pleased to have a staff of nurses forced upon him. Nor did he want nurses with prior alcohol and drug treatment experience. He decided he was only going to hire nurses who lived in the area for at least three years and he was going to hire them at ridiculously low salaries.

There I was, no job, no home, no prospect of getting a job in that tiny town. Almost out of money, I knew no one. All I had to my name were my car and the clothes I'd brought with me. I never felt so alone in my life. I called the local Unity Church and told my story to the minister.

As a way out of this mess, she and I formed a Mastermind group. We began to look at things from the spiritual level rather than the human level.

The Miracle Portal

Where there was an appearance of unemployment we began to declare that my true job was expressing the Mastermind in every way I could.

Where there was an appearance of lack of a home we declared that my true home was in the Mastermind.

Where there was a lack of money and food we declared that the Mastermind provides for all the needs of Its children *at every moment*.

We declared that I was living like the children of Israel in the wilderness, for whom day by day the mana fell.

Within one week I had a part-time nursing job in an area where jobs of any type were very difficult to find. A total stranger took me into her home and I lived with this dear lady for about six weeks while I got back on my feet. More strangers asked my advice on dealing with loved ones who were chemically dependent and insisted I accept either food or money for my trouble. My car was repaired twice at no cost by strangers who stopped to help me on the side of the road. (One helper was named Mr. Love, I'll never forget him.)

Nancy Reynolds

The most important lesson I learned was, the Mastermind loves us and will provide for us at all times and in all situations if we will turn to It with complete faith and the knowledge that the human picture is an illusion. The Mastermind's complete and abundant universe is the truth.

When people think about the miracles from the Bible, they often believe the miracles happened to 'special' people. Readers suppose miracles were created by a Mastermind who loved one person or group of people so much that especially for them It suspended Its own laws of the universe.

The truth is the biblical miracles were accomplished because a spiritually minded person (or often a group of people) saw through the illusion of evil and thereby brought the reality of good into their experience.

These people were no more special than you or I. They saw a problem and knew that somehow they had to overcome the human picture and see through the illusion if they wanted to solve it. So they asked the Mastermind to help them see things as they truly were, not as they appeared to be.

The Miracle Portal

These early seekers of truth denied the testimony of their physical senses and instead insisted that the Mastermind created everything that was ever created and it was all good.

As they consistently held their thoughts and feelings to what they knew through faith was real spiritually, the reality of good appeared.

Then as they began to physically see an unveiling on the physical plane, they gained more confidence. The more confidence they had the more faith they had. Very soon all that was left for them to behold, even on the physical plane, was the good -- the reality of the universe created by the Mastermind. *They experienced a miracle.*

A good example of this is in the parting of the Red Sea when the Israelites were fleeing from the Egyptians. (Exodus 13:17-14:31). Many of the Israelites had little faith in the concept of God. They'd lived as slaves in Egypt for so long they'd begun worshipping the Egyptian gods. Their main goal in leaving Egypt was to get out of slavery. They were definitely looking at things from the human level.

Following Moses out to the middle of the desert, they looked back and saw the entire Egyptian army in hot pursuit. They turned on Moses saying, "It would have been better for us to serve the Egyptians than to die in the desert." (Exodus 14:2).

However, Moses believed in the Mastermind. Moses saw things from the spiritual level and because he did, he refused to acknowledge the human picture. He didn't know how the Mastermind was going to save them. Moses only knew they would be saved. He told the children of Israel, "Do not be afraid. Stand firm and you will see the deliverance the Lord will bring you today. The Egyptians you see today you will never see again. The Lord will fight for you. You need only to be still." (Exodus 14:15-16).

Moses listened to his spiritual sense. He prayed about the problem and the 'still small voice' of the Mastermind spoke to him. No great thundering voice came down from heaven and spoke aloud, but within himself, his inner voice said, "Why are you crying out to me? Tell the Israelites to move on. Raise your staff and stretch

The Miracle Portal

out your hand over the sea to divide the water so that the Israelites can go through the sea on dry ground." (Exodus 14:15-18).

How outrageous can you get! Pursued by the entire Egyptian army, Moses hears an inner voice that says, "It's okay, just raise your staff over the water and part this sea so the people can walk across this submerged land bridge I led you to."

Think about this. If we don't live in a playground where we have dominion and physical laws are responsive to our thoughts, then the laws of the universe were completely reversed in this one instance to protect the children of Israel.

Most people find such a thought violates their common sense. If we live in a world where we have dominion over supposed physical laws, then one man with an absolute belief in the power of the Mastermind can make the illusions of this world conform to his will. And that's exactly what Moses did. He didn't question the absurdity of the situation. He moved on and did what his spiritual sense told him to do. The waters parted, a submerged land bridge appeared, and the children of Israel walked through on dry land.

Notice that Moses didn't try to do this on his own. He didn't take credit for parting the Red Sea. It's a combination of power: the Mastermind and our belief in the power of the Mastermind which changes the physical picture.

I've heard the story of a modern-day Red Sea. A woman who lives in the Midwest was a victim of a flood. She stood in the doorway of her house watching the waters rise all around her. Her house was on higher ground but the water rose insidiously until it was lapping at her front doorstep. At that point, in desperation, she cried out with absolute conviction, "No, God!" And the water stopped. There was flooding all around the property. She lost the barn, but the water did not come inside her house.

We live in a responsive universe. The Mastermind created it that way for us. When Moses parted the Red Sea, or Joshua caused the walls of Jericho to fall, or Elijah caused the widow's oil to multiply, or Daniel survived the lion's den, or Jesus walked on water, or Peter's shadow healed people, it was because they knew how to appeal to the spiritual laws of the universe which supersede physical laws.

Miracles are not a matter of bringing the supernatural into the real world. Miracles are a matter of bringing the real and perfect world created by the Mastermind into a world of illusions. *Miracles are the fulfillment of spiritual law.*

We are told to, "Judge not by appearances but judge righteous judgment." (John 7:24). The Mastermind is always willing and anxious to help Its children see through illusions to the underlying reality.

So does this mean I have to have the kind of faith Jesus or Moses had to get a miracle?

Jesus said, "If you have faith as small as a mustard seed you can say to this mountain move from here to there and it will move. Nothing will be impossible for you." (Matthew 17:20-22).

He meant literal mountains and he meant figurative mountains of illness and strife and lack. And how much faith was that? As tiny as a mustard seed? Do you remember how tiny that is? When I was a little girl there were charms made of a mustard seed enclosed in plastic. A mustard seed is about the size of the head of a pin.

So Jesus proposed to pit the piddly faith of a mustard seed against a mountain?

Yes, he did. Because he knew that as children of the Mastermind even a speck of faith was enough to totally alter things on the physical plane, which is nothing but a world of illusion.

There is no order of difficulty in miracles because one illusion is as easy to erase as another. The difficulty is in the human mind of the beholder.

For instance, someone may find it easy to believe that poverty is an illusion and so he easily demonstrates the Mastermind's good and produces abundance. But illness --- ooh --- illness is real! So try as he might, he cannot see through the illusion of illness into health.

Almost everyone finds it easier to see through some things and harder to see through others. Isn't it wonderful that the Mastermind has provided us with friends, Mastermind partners who can see for us what we struggle to see for ourselves?

Remember, even one person perceiving the truth about a situation will bring a demonstration of the truth into the physical plane. One person knowing the truth will bring into physical evidence the good the Mastermind has already created. The evil will disappear into its native nothingness.

What is the activity of the Mastermind and how does it take place in me?

The activity of the Mastermind is love, the ultimate vibration of good. It takes place in you when you let your thoughts and emotions be ruled by thoughts and feelings of love.

In truth, there never was a moment when your thoughts and feelings were separate from the Mastermind's. In a world of human illusions, we often feel we are separated. This step might better read, "I believe that the activity of the Mastermind is now and always has been taking place in me."

If the activity of the Mastermind were not taking place in you, if the Mastermind were not maintaining the perfect creative idea of you, you would not exist. By this, I don't mean that you'd be dead. (The truth is there is no death, there is only a change in experience from the physical to the spiritual.) If the Mastermind were not maintaining the perfect creative thought about you, you would not exist here on Earth, in the spiritual realm, or anywhere else!

Fortunately, you can't cease to exist because the Mastermind created and maintains you. "God is the same yesterday and today and forever." (Hebrews 13:8).

We need to acknowledge and consciously use what has always been the truth by aligning our thoughts and feelings as closely as we can to the Mastermind's standard of perfect good.

There really is a power greater than yourself, a Mastermind power that has created and completed a universe of perfect sanity, order, goodness, and beauty. The Mastermind is constantly using avenues of thought and feeling to remind you of Its presence and love for you.

How is the Mastermind's sanity and order working within me now?

_____

_____

_____

The Miracle Portal

CHAPTER SEVEN

Step Four

I make a decision to place my will and my life under the care and guidance of the Mastermind.

Why should I turn my will and life over to anyone but myself?

Let me ask, are you doing such a great job with your life? Because if you are, if you really believe that your life doesn't need at least a change, why are you reading this book? If you're convinced you don't need help to run your life, you may be missing out on the Kingdom of Heaven.

And what is the Kingdom of Heaven? It's that level of thought and feeling where you realize your oneness with the Mastermind and all that oneness entails. It is the realm of the Mastermind and it is right here, right now.

So your decision to turn your will and life over to the care and guidance of the Mastermind indicates you acknowledge that you need help from your Creator. You are teachable and willing to let the Mastermind take over and guide you. You admit that the Mastermind can see what you cannot.

I've seen people struggle with the idea of turning their will and life over to a Higher Power. But I've also seen the rewards that come to those who have surrendered their lives to the Mastermind.

I had a colleague who was a fine nurse and helped me enormously when I was learning cardiac nursing. Because of my background in chemical dependency treatment, I was one of only a few people who knew this man had a serious problem with an addiction to narcotics. He had already lost his nursing license once but he had been through treatment and was now completing his probationary program as a recovering nurse.

After about a year of working together, I left the unit we were on and went to another hospital. Unfortunately, my colleague had problems with the stress of his work and the constant temptation of narcotic medications. He relapsed and his nursing license was revoked again when he was caught stealing narcotics from the hospital.

Several weeks after this happened, he called to tell me about the trouble he was in and to ask if I knew anyone who would let him work as a nurse's aide or orderly. I said I didn't know of any work, but I would be happy to Mastermind with him.

Even though he'd been an AA Member, he'd never heard of a Mastermind group. He had no real interest in joining one. He didn't want to turn his will and life over to the Mastermind, but he was desperate so he agreed. It took several months for him to begin to forgive himself, but because of the support of the Mastermind, he could see that nursing was not a good career choice.

He began to understand the problems that led to his drug addiction in ways he had never understood before. Soon, because he placed his will and his life under the direction of the Mastermind, he found himself working in a very satisfactory job that did not involve nursing or the temptation of drugs. Most important, he had a new source of spiritual understanding and support in his life.

What is the care and guidance of the Mastermind?

Obviously, the guidance of the Mastermind will be different for each individual. But the care of the Mastermind is unchanging.

You are the Mastermind's beloved child. What could be better than the care of all the good and power in the universe? And what better guide could you possibly have than All-Knowing Love?

How do I know the Mastermind will make the right decisions for me?

I love this question! How could All-Knowing Good possibly make the wrong decisions for you? This question crosses our minds because we get the Mastermind confused with the idea of our human parents.

Our parents loved us in their way. They did the best they could for us, given their human limitations. As we mature we realize they're living in the same illusions we are, believing in their separate human minds. Because they are, they make decisions and judgments about us that sometimes have nothing to do with who *we* are.

Those decisions and judgments are really about who *they* are. In the end, decisions made for us and about us by our human parents can turn out to be hurtful and destructive.

We have a right to fight against turning our will and lives, our decisions and plans over to any other human being no matter who they are.

On the other hand, the Mastermind is our Creator. It is our only true parent. Its decisions and judgments are absolutely based on *our* needs. The Mastermind knows all the secret desires of our hearts and It agrees with them. It knows every good quality we have.

The not-so-good qualities? The Mastermind's only desire is to heal the misperceptions that led to those qualities in the first place. An important fact to remember: The Mastermind's healing is not painful. The Mastermind's healing is a release from pain.

Cast out any fear you may have about letting the Mastermind control your life. The Mastermind's will for you is absolute good. It wants you to have whatever you desire. The

The Miracle Portal

Mastermind will fulfill the desires of your heart if you will only surrender.

What is your greatest fear about relinquishing control to the Mastermind?

_____

_____

_____

_____

_____

_____

_____

_____

_____

_____

_____

_____

_____

_____

_____

_____

Chapter Eight

Step Five

I release all anger, resentment, guilt, and blame I've felt towards anyone I've ever known. I release them and let them go. I sincerely ask forgiveness of anyone I may have hurt or offended. I also release myself from all guilt and blame. I forgive.

Why should I release those who have hurt or wronged me from my anger, resentment, and blame?

This seems to be the step with which everyone beginning Masterminding has the hardest time. There are a multitude of reasons for this step, but let's look first at the one that has the most meaning to you right now: *if you don't forgive you will never progress in the Mastermind Process*. Not forgiving will block your good from coming to you. That's the bottom line. If you want to get what you want, you must forgive. What is more valuable? Your grudge or your desire?

Even if every fiber of your being strains against forgiving that one unforgivable person, remind yourself that you don't know everything yet, and if you want to get your heart's desire you must forgive.

Let's say I want to forgive. How can I? I can't forgive some of these people for what they've done. I've tried and I just can't.

Some illusions of this world seem so real, and some of them seem so hurtful you can't work up the *feeling* of forgiveness. What's needed here is a willingness to forgive. If you go to the Mastermind saying, "I haven't been able to feel forgiveness towards this person on my own, but I am willing to forgive. Please help me." You'll find the forgiveness process will begin immediately.

I have a wonderful spiritual teacher, Edwene Gaines, who tells this story each time she does a prosperity workshop. (Gaines lecture, Prosperity Plus.) It's the best forgiveness story I've ever heard, so I hope she won't mind if I borrow it to illustrate this point.

Edween began her career as an English teacher. She loved to travel. She signed up to teach for the State Department in Guam. One of the reasons she agreed to teach in Guam was because, at the end of a two-year contract, the government offered a trip around the world. While she was in Guam Edween got married. Their contracts ran simultaneously so they went together on their trip around the world.

Edween was six months pregnant. She was very happy with her life and marriage and was having a wonderful time on her trip. Until one night in Hong Kong when her husband announced to her, "Edween, I don't love you anymore and I'm leaving." He took both their airline tickets and all their money. And Edween says, "If you've ever tried to get a job in Hong Kong when you're six months pregnant, you know what a challenge is."

She finally made it back to the United States, but she was "very angry." She was convinced, "Life was unfair and men were no good." She lived the next nine years of her life "in rage." And as she says, "That's a terrible place to live."

The Miracle Portal

She became terminally ill with cancer and was given six months to live when she said, "I knew I had to forgive but I didn't know how. So I began to pray and my prayer went something like this: I forgive you, you sorry so and so!" After a while, Edween said, she began to feel some understanding and compassion for her ex-husband. Now, she says the forgiveness process is complete. The most important thing is, her rage and sickness of soul disappeared along with the cancer. Forgiveness can save your life.

I've seen this proven repeatedly with myself and my Mastermind partners. Be willing and ask for help from the Mastermind. Even if you can only say through gritted teeth as Edween did, "I forgive you, you sorry so and so." If you are willing to ask the Mastermind for help, your healing will begin.

Healing through forgiveness may not happen overnight. Some of us have pretty deep-seated grudges. Some of us have a lot of people in our lives to forgive. What seemed impossible will become possible. The more you are willing to forgive, the more you will forgive, until the healing is complete.

You'll also find that when you've worked sufficiently on the forgiveness process, so all those awful feelings you buried in your heart are forgiven, you'll feel about a hundred pounds lighter and one hundred percent freer.

You'll come to understand unforgiveness is a punishment you heap on yourself. It doesn't affect the person you begrudge at all.

In the future when hurts come up you'll start to work immediately on forgiveness. Imagine releasing that heavy burden.

Don't try to do this without the Mastermind. Don't try to sugarcoat your feelings of unforgiveness and brush them under the rug. If you do you'll only be repressing them, not healing them. Take your feelings of anger, resentment, guilt, and blame to the Mastermind and let them be healed, not whitewashed.

Does forgiving people mean I have to be their friend? Do I have to pretend to like them?

No. There's a big difference between forgiving someone and wanting to be their friend. It's not even necessary to physically talk with the person you're forgiving. Often you can't talk to them because they're dead. Others may live in an unknown area. Some remain emotionally unreachable.

Forgiveness happens on a spiritual level. You can go to the person you need to forgive in your mind and acknowledge they are the child of the Mastermind just as you are. You can acknowledge the truth about them and the situation, the Mastermind never created a child who could harm another one of Its children in any way. The appearance of their harming you is an illusion and on that basis, you can forgive.

Never mind the material picture, never mind the litany of complaints your human mind has against this person. Release the person you need to forgive and go about your business doing your best to live in love. If your human mind re-introduces its complaints about this person, remind yourself you have forgiven them on a spiritual basis. Keep holding to the truth about them and your forgiveness process will reach completion.

You may find after you are done you will become friends, or you may never see them again. What's important is, you have blessed them by knowing the truth about them.

Sometimes I find it easier to forgive others than to forgive myself. How do I release myself from all guilt and blame?

Use the same process you used in forgiving another person. You say to the Mastermind, "I haven't been able to forgive myself for doing this, but I'm willing to forgive. Please help me." The Mastermind's help will come just as immediately on your behalf as it did on behalf of another.

Let me warn you, as you begin the forgiveness process on yourself your human mind will put up a tremendous racket. It will be sure to remind you of all the reasons you should not be forgiven. Turn your attention away from these thoughts. They are not the truth.

Does forgiving myself mean I don't have to take responsibility for my actions?

You asked the Mastermind to forgive you for something, which It has already done. You asked the Mastermind to help you forgive yourself. It does so. How long do you think your self-forgiveness will last if, the next time you're tempted, you repeat the same mistake?

We must work to understand the mistakes for which we ask forgiveness. We strive to correct our faults and not repeat them. If correction is your desire, the Mastermind will help with that too.

Forgiveness for yourself and others is an essential part of the Mastermind Process. Without it, you will struggle and sweat to get your heart's desire. With it, you will claim your heart's desire with ease and joy. You will grow spiritually and become free.

The Mastermind can do for you what you cannot do for yourself. Take your feelings of unforgiveness to the Mastermind, ask for help, and see this awful burden taken from you.

Are you willing to release all anger, resentment, guilt, and blame?

The Miracle Portal

Chapter Nine

Step Six

I humbly ask the Mastermind to take complete control of my life and to change *me* knowing that if I am changed everything in my life will be different in a corresponding way.

Why will everything in my life be different if I'm different?

This is one of the most important points in Masterminding. The truth is *everything* starts inside you. Your world is made up of your thoughts about it.

If you want your world to change you *must* change yourself, your thoughts, and your feelings. Again, this is a spiritual principle: *as within so without.*

Every spiritual path on the planet teaches this principle. Our outer world is dependent on our inner world.

Well, what things about me need to be changed?

I don't know. You may not know. A good place to start is to ask yourself about your negative traits. Are you a negative person? Do you tend to look for the good or the bad in people and situations? (Don't be too hard on yourself about this. In this material world, we're trained to look for the negative rather than the positive.) *Do you do unto others as you would have them do unto you?*

Be very gentle with yourself when asking these questions. None of us are perfect yet. But it's important to begin today to correct those things about ourselves which are not in harmony with all good.

You're living in a world of illusions. You may have no idea what things in you need to be changed to bring about your heart's desire.

I suggest that what you do not know, the Mastermind does. *Ask the Mastermind.* Get quiet and ask, "What must I change about myself, my thinking and feeling, to receive my desire?"

Sometimes the Mastermind will get through to you in very obvious ways. Sometimes, usually out of fear, you'll block the response. But the changes will have begun because you asked for them.

Well if I don't know what changes need to be made how can I work on them?

Sometimes your effort is required. The Mastermind will let you know. Other times because you've asked for a healing, the Mastermind does Its work. If there's something in your belief system or personality that's bothering you, ask for healing in that area. Then work as diligently as you can to correct that unwanted trait.

If you don't know what needs healing, simply ask that whatever internal blocks are standing in your way be removed. The Mastermind will tell you everything you need to know.

How will the Mastermind change me?

It will change your thoughts and feelings, which are the basis for everything. It will change your beliefs or attitudes or superstitions or whatever is keeping you from expressing your highest good.

The Miracle Portal

I had to do serious work to release my personal negativity and judgment of others. I tried my best daily to refrain from thinking negatively. I had to acknowledge that I often judge others, and I had to stop that. I still work on this every single day, but now it's much easier than it used to be.

After working on this, something curious has happened. I find myself much more sensitive to the needs and feelings of other people. I have become sensitive to such a degree that I have a hard time watching television because so much of it is negative and violent. Similarly, I now avoid many magazine and newspaper articles because I see no redeeming information in them. They seem to glorify negativity and violence. It seems the news media is intent on hyping fear.

I've also learned that sarcasm is assassination. Criticizing is murder. The same thoughts and emotions that lead to ill humor also lead to killing. Both infuriation and murder are a condemnation of our brothers and sisters to greater or lesser degrees. We're also pretty good at assassinating ourselves. These negative thoughts and emotions poison our environment and everyone around us.

Trust the Mastermind to know everything about you that needs to be changed. You only have to be willing to change and to cooperate with the changes taking place in you.

Are you willing to ask the Mastermind to change your heart and mind?

_____
_____
_____
_____

What must I change about myself to receive my desire?

_____
_____
_____
_____
_____
_____
_____
_____
_____

The Miracle Portal

My thinking?

My feelings?

Chapter Ten

Step Seven

I now share my need or desire with my Mastermind group.

Masterminding should not be used only to acquire things. Make your request, but understand every time you make a demonstration you've had a change of consciousness to go with it.

There are a variety of demonstrations; a material need or desire met, a physical healing, a relationship healed, or a personality fault corrected.

For these things to happen, you had a change in your thoughts and feelings. Otherwise, you would never have made the demonstration.

In our group, we've come to regard demonstrations as the gold stars of the Mastermind. I don't mean that in a flippant way. We're enormously grateful for those gold stars. They're indications that we have grown spiritually and have a new command of spiritual principles.

It's sometimes difficult to know what your *true* desires are because of the illusions of the world. However, there are some things we can know about true versus false desires. A true desire *benefits everyone*. A true desire does not infringe upon the rights of anyone else.

You cannot use the Mastermind process to change another person against their will. You could ask for harmony in a relationship. You could ask that a situation be worked out for the highest good of all concerned. But you cannot childishly demand that someone else meet your expectations.

For instance, you may desire to find a loving person to share your life and be your mate. That is a desire that would benefit everyone and infringe upon no one. However, if you insist that you want one specific person to be your mate, no one else will do, that is a false desire. The person you want might have other plans.

It may take some practice to learn to purify your desires, to look at the situation, and make sure you are not infringing on the rights of others. But the rewards are great. The person you were sure you wanted may not have been the one for you. In in your human limitation, you may not have realized that. The Mastermind with Its superior vision of the whole knows just the person to meet your needs.

There is no competition in the Universe. The Mastermind makes sure everyone gets exactly what they need without disturbing anyone else's plan.

Therefore, if you ask for a specific job know that if the job is meant to be yours it will be. You will not take it from another. If you get it, it was never meant to be theirs. If that is not the right job for you, if you wait, never doubting, you will be led to the one that best benefits you.

Remember the law of non-competition when you ask for a need or desire. If you are tempted to feel competitive with anyone, wish good for them instead. Put your thoughts and feelings to work for the highest good for all concerned.

In this step, as each Mastermind partner shares their need or desire with the group, every other group member gives an affirmation that their partner's need is met.

Try to limit your needs and desires to no more than two each week. As you'll see later, your

Mastermind partners commit to holding the vision for you and your desires during the week. More than two desires become hard to accommodate.

Imagine I said to my Mastermind group, "I have a large insurance payment coming up and I don't have the money to pay the bill. I need to have that bill taken care of."

Tina might affirm for me, "The Mastermind knows you have these worldly matters to handle. It knows you need this payment made. Because you have asked for Its help, the means for making that payment is now on its way to you."

Carol might add her affirmation and say, "It's right that you have the protection of insurance. And it's right that the people who provide the service to you should be paid cheerfully and on time. The Mastermind has arranged it so that what benefits one benefits all. I know for you this need will be met on time and with ease."

Christie might conclude by saying, "The Mastermind knows what your insurance payment is. I affirm for you that It meets this need with Its energy in the form of money, just as It causes grass to grow and rain to feed the earth."

I can guarantee after multiple experiences and demonstrations if such a request is made in a Mastermind group, the payment will be worked out.

You can have anything you want if you believe you can. Material objects are playtoys on the physical plane of existence. You can have any playtoy you want.

If that's true then why does one person drive a Rolls Royce and another person drive a twenty-year-old Toyota?

The person with the Rolls Royce wanted it, believed they could have it, and spent time and energy imagining and feeling it was theirs.

Maybe the person with the Toyota aspired to this Toyota. Or, maybe the person with a Toyota doesn't believe they deserve better.

The person who desires a luxury car may believe they can have it, but they don't understand how to follow spiritual principles to bring it into their life.

Everything we have in our lives reflects our beliefs and desires. To manifest a material object or anything else on the physical plane we must desire it, we must feel the thrill of receiving it, and we must imagine it with the belief that we have it *now*.

Some people desire material objects more than others. That doesn't make one person better or holier than another. Some people need to learn material possessions don't bring happiness. As long as you know that happiness comes from within no matter what material objects you possess, you may begin to enliven your life with the types of material objects you enjoy.

Material objects, including money, are really nothing more than the out-picturing of your thoughts, feelings, and beliefs. They are like the silly putty and tinker toys of the Universe. You can have all the silly putty you want. Never be too shy to ask for any material object or any sum of money. Just be sure you never hurt another person in getting it.

Don't let the desire for things or money become the overriding preoccupation of your life. It is an *obsession with money*, not the money itself, that is the root of all evil. Remember our real goal in Masterminding is to grow spiritually.

Manifesting physical healing is not unlike manifesting material objects although because of our culture, we think healing the sick is much more spiritual. Physical healing is a complicated and controversial subject. I make no recommendations about how any individual should pursue theirs.

As a Registered Nurse, I believe in the merits of medical treatment while at the same time acknowledging its limitations. The fact that we treat the human body medically, just as we repair our cars, does not negate the law. If physical healing ever occurred by spiritual practice it means that all healing is possible through spiritual practice. The Mastermind does not suspend the laws of the universe to heal one special person and let others suffer on their own.

In my experience, physical healings have occurred in several different ways through Masterminding. I've seen people led to exactly the right physician. I've seen people healed simply by asking for help in their Mastermind group. I've seen people led to non-traditional healers.

In every case, the Mastermind knew exactly where they needed to go to receive the healing they requested. Physical healing is just another way in which the Mastermind meets our needs and desires. If you're especially interested in healing there are many fine books and lectures on the subject. Some of them are listed in the suggested reading at the end of this book.

In asking for your desires you must also practice a certain amount of patience and detachment. Patience is necessary because the Mastermind often has to effect a change in you, in your thinking, feeling, or beliefs, before you're ready to receive your desire.

Detachment is necessary because, though we try not to insist on a specific form of our desires, we do sometimes get in our own way and slow down the receiving process. Sometimes you limit yourself and the Mastermind by insisting on the form your desire should take.

If you are willing for your good to come to you in unlimited and unexpected ways, you will be pleasantly surprised at how perfectly the Mastermind will work things out on your behalf.

Never be afraid to let the Mastermind make the final selection. In the end, it will work more perfectly than anything you could have imagined.

Another reason detachment is needed is that sometimes we become anxious about our desires. Anxiety is another form of fear, which slows down the demonstration of our good. Maybe the human situation you're dealing with appears quite serious and you have a lot of fear about not getting your need met.

Remember, fear is the enemy. Release your fear to the healing of the Mastermind. Believe It loves you and will meet your need.

The Mastermind can assist you and started to work on your desire before you even asked for help.

- Be clear about what you want.
- State your desire.
- Imagine yourself receiving it.
- Feel what it would be like to have it.
- Expect to get it.

Realize the Mastermind meets all your needs and desires because It loves you. Let your

The Miracle Portal

Mastermind group help you by believing on your behalf. Release any feelings of anxiety or competition. Detach, and watch miracles happen.

What is your first desire?

_____

_____

_____

_____

_____

_____

Can you accept that the Mastermind wants something better for you than you wanted for yourself?

_____

_____

_____

_____

_____

_____

CHAPTER ELEVEN
Step Eight

I express my faith in the power of the Mastermind and I give thanks that it is done. Thank you, Mastermind, it is done! My life is dramatically changed. The Mastermind and I are now partners.

I want to have faith but how do I know I have enough faith? I mean, even if I do believe the Mastermind holds all the power in the universe, I'm still not sure the Mastermind will use it to help me.

I spoke earlier of faith the size of a mustard seed being enough to move mountains of trouble, sickness, and lack. When they begin to Mastermind, many people have only a smidgen of faith. In fact, they may have more hope than faith -- they hope someone is telling them the truth about the miracles they can receive. Faith doesn't happen until they see the Mastermind's love in action.

In the Bible, we see, "Faith is the substance of things hoped for, the evidence of things not seen." (Hebrews 2:1).

That means faith [expectancy] brings desires out of the invisible realm of spirit (the only real substance in the universe) and manifests them on the physical plane.

You may have found, as I have, that faith, belief, and fear are all tied up together in human thinking.

Faith and belief are very similar and are listed as synonyms in the thesaurus. But faith is stronger than belief. When you are in faith you are under the protection of the Mastermind and you are seeing what's real spiritually even though you may not yet see it with your human eyes.

We might even say that faith is belief in action. If you truly have faith in something, you believe it so strongly that you take action on it. You have faith that the sun is going to come up tomorrow, so you take action today to do the wash. You'll need something to wear to work in the morning.

You have faith that Los Angeles is in California, so when you plan a trip to Los Angeles you plan for stops along the way to California, not Kansas. Faith is absolute conviction.

Fear is the opposite of faith and it is the opposite of love. Therefore, fear is the opposite of the Mastermind.

If there were a devil it would be fear. Fear is only an invention of the human mind. When you are in fear you are at the mercy of the human mind. You are believing:

False
Evidence
Appearing
Real

Every spiritual teacher has confronted the false belief of fear. A father asked Jesus to heal his son who suffered from severe epilepsy since childhood. Jesus told them to bring the boy to him and then turned to the father. "Jesus said to him, 'If you can believe, all things are possible to him who believes.' And the father of the child cried out, and said with tears, 'Lord I believe. Help me overcome my unbelief.'" (Mark 9:23-25). Of course, the story has a happy ending. The boy was healed. Jesus was obviously willing and able to strengthen the man's belief because he was asked. It was a miracle or the natural outworking of love.

What this lovely humble man said to Jesus is what we all often feel and say with tears in our own eyes. "I believe in part and I want to believe completely, but I'm afraid. Please help the part of me that's afraid."

We have modern miracles too. Because we ask, the Mastermind adds strength to the part of us that's afraid.

The Mastermind's love will multiply our faith and make us strong if we ask for help. Very soon our desires will be met and our faith will increase. It will continue to increase until like Jesus, we can say, "Whatever you ask for in prayer believe that you have received it and it will be yours." (Mark 2:24).

How can I give thanks that my desire is met before I actually see it?

Because your desire, imagination, and expectancy (faith) are pulling it out of the unseen spiritual substance and into the physical world. Your expression of thanks is an acknowledgment and affirmation that you understand spiritual principle.

Maharishi Mahesh Yogi gave thanks that he and his followers would soon be housed in a new building. When asked where his organization would get the money to buy a new building, he said, "From wherever it is at the moment."

He understood the money to build his building was waiting in the unseen spiritual substance of the universe to be called upon. Once called, it would manifest itself on the physical plane. The Maharishi was right. He got the money to build his building.

Charles Fillmore started the Unity building fund with one penny. He said, "The inexhaustible resource of spirit is equal to every demand. There is no reality in lack. Abundance is here and now manifest."

Not only was the Unity Church quickly built, but today Unity School of Christianity is a worldwide ministry with a huge and lovely main campus in Lees Summit, Missouri.

The Miracle Portal

Jesus knew and told his disciples days before he would raise Lazarus from the dead. When Jesus stood with the crowd outside the tomb, Lazarus had already been dead for four days. The people could not imagine Jesus would attempt to raise a man from the dead who had lain in his tomb for four days.

The first thing Jesus did was thank the Mastermind for meeting his need. "Then Jesus looked up and said, 'Father I thank you that you have heard me. I knew that you hear me always, but I said this for the benefit of the people standing here, that they may believe that you sent me.'" (John 11:41-43).

And of course, we know the rest of the story. Lazarus came forth from the tomb alive.

In the past when I've needed money I've turned to the Mastermind and said again and again, "Thank you, you know my need." Rather than trying to figure out how the money would manifest, whenever I started to worry about the situation I would say again, "Thank you for meeting my need." And the money always turned up, sometimes in astounding ways. One time I received a large insurance refund on a policy I didn't even know I had.

The Mastermind has endless ways of bringing your good to you, so don't worry about how it's going to happen this time. Say thank you for the Mastermind's help and expect to receive more.

What does it mean to be partners with the Mastermind?

It means you are co-creating your world with the Mastermind. The Mastermind gave you free will, and for years you may have been using free will to run your life from the human level -- getting some good results and some bad.

How wonderful to know you can leave the human level and move to the spiritual level to co-create with the Mastermind by asking that it be so and then following the spiritual principles that allow it to happen.

Every Mastermind group member will encourage you to have faith in the power of the Mastermind. Its power is unfailing.

- Affirm your faith.

- Call your desires into physical manifestation.
- Thank the Mastermind for Its assistance before you see the results physically.
- Expect to get what you desire.
- Act as if it's already yours because, in the realm of spirit, it is.

Can you give examples of the Mastermind's power?

_____
_____
_____
_____
_____
_____
_____
_____
_____
_____
_____

___

___

___

How did you feel when you saw the evidence of the Mastermind's love for you?

___

___

___

___

___

___

___

___

___

___

___

___

___

___

The Miracle Portal

What fear can the Mastermind help you overcome?

Chapter Twelve
Step Nine

I commit myself to hold the vision daily for my Mastermind partners.

How do I hold the vision for my Mastermind partners?

Think about your partners frequently throughout the day. Mentally see them achieving their desires. Affirm that their desires are already met. In this way, you see through the illusion of the human mind and declare the truth of the situation.

Let's say one of your Mastermind partners brought the need for relationship healing at work to the Mastermind group. In holding the vision for them you might say, "I know the Mastermind created all of Its children to express good. Therefore, this person who seems to be behaving so badly toward my Mastermind partner is truly their friend. This person is just as loving as my partner. They may be caught in fear right now (the only reason anyone behaves unlovingly) but the Mastermind is now in charge of this situation. The Mastermind shows everyone how to resolve the situation for the highest good of all involved. I support my Mastermind partner in their efforts to see the highest good for everyone."

Then you might say, "I affirm that we are all displaying love and harmony in all our affairs. My thoughts, and the thoughts of my Mastermind partner, are now being healed of any thinking that falls short of love. Love is the only reality for everyone involved in this situation."

Imagine for a few moments how everyone involved in your partner's situation is becoming aware of their mutual harmony. Imagine the many ways in which a new loving attitude is changing everything.

Use the same steps for your partner that you use for yourself when manifesting a need or desire. Desire the best outcome for everyone involved. Imagine it and expect it to happen. Believe for your partner what they have difficulty believing for themselves.

Hold the vision for your Mastermind partners every day until your next Mastermind meeting. At the meeting, you get to hear all about the miracles appearing in their lives during the past week. Sometimes it takes more than a week for your partner's needs to manifest, sometimes it takes less. The healing will always come.

Meanwhile, your Mastermind partners are holding the vision for you. During the next meeting, you get to share your miracles with them.

How hard is it to think about someone else's desires while I'm thinking of mine?

_____
_____
_____
_____

This is the spiritual law of giving and receiving love. How good am I about receiving love?

_____
_____
_____

The Miracle Portal

How generous am I at giving love to my Mastermind partner(s)?

Chapter Thirteen
How It's Done

Each Mastermind group does things a little differently. I'll tell you the general rules of the process and refer to some of the different ways Mastermind meetings are conducted.

Time and Place

Your Mastermind meeting should be held at the same time and place every week. Meetings may be held in individual homes, restaurants, meeting rooms, churches, or anywhere your group feels comfortable.

Our group holds meetings by Zoom because not everyone lives in the same town. We find the results are just as good. The Mastermind doesn't know about time and space -- those are human concepts.

There should be discipline and commitment in your Masterminding. I've observed that those who make the strongest commitment and look forward to Masterminding with the greatest enthusiasm also have the biggest demonstrations.

Selecting Mastermind Group Members

What are the qualities to look for in my Mastermind partners?

Mastermind partners can be family members, personal friends, friendly acquaintances, or perfect strangers. Anyone interested in being a Mastermind partner must have a willingness to believe in a Higher Power. That's the number one requirement in selecting Mastermind partners.

Your Mastermind partners must also believe they need help in achieving their needs and desires. Your partners must have experienced trying to run their lives, getting some good results and some bad, and be willing to try another way. Once a partner's needs are met that doesn't mean their time and energy aren't needed by the other group members.

Anyone who uses Masterminding purely to get things will find they stop getting demonstrations because they've stopped growing spiritually.

Sometimes a well-intentioned person will drop out of the group because they just can't surrender to one or more of the spiritual laws.

I've seen people who absolutely refuse to forgive others. Their demonstrations are limited because they refuse to forgive.

I've seen people refuse to surrender their will and their lives to the care and guidance of the Mastermind. In that case, they are not ready for the Mastermind Process.

This isn't a judgment against these people. They are seekers of truth. Everyone must grow in their way and time.

You'll know when a partner can no longer grow in your group. They'll start missing meetings, making excuses for why they can't attend, why they're running late, etc. Don't try to convince them to stay. Love them and release them. The Mastermind will always take care of them.

How many partners should be in my group?

The ideal number of Mastermind partners is between two and six. It's a good idea to have no more than six because you are responsible for holding the daily vision for each Mastermind partner.

If you have pioneered a group and you get more than six, split them up into different areas. Good for you!

It's a little difficult to do justice to more than six people. Also, as we look at the actual structure of the Mastermind meeting you'll see more than six would be extremely time-consuming.

The Structure of the Mastermind Meeting

Your Mastermind meeting should have a leader. It may be the same person each week or leadership can rotate among the group members. It's the leader's job to read each Mastermind step as the meeting progresses.

Mastermind meetings usually begin with each partner telling about the progress they've seen in their need or desire, or their spiritual growth. They also give thanks to the Mastermind.

After everyone shares their stories, each group may do things differently.

One group has a very formal meeting with linen tablecloths and candlelight. They start their meeting by reading inspirational texts and then go on to meditate. After that, they begin the Mastermind steps.

Another group begins with a meditation and then goes on with the steps.

My group goes right to the steps with no stops in between. Do whatever feels right to you.

Utilizing the Steps

Again, different groups utilize the steps in slightly different ways. In our group, we use the following format.

The group leader reads each step aloud and then tells their feelings about it. The next group member adds their feelings, and so forth.

In our group, we often get into discussions regarding the spiritual principles in the various steps. For instance, Tina might be having a challenge with forgiveness, so Carol, Christie, and I would lend her support with statements of spiritual truth and suggestions we were led to give by the Mastermind. We might tell her about a similar challenge we faced and what spiritual means helped us to overcome it.

A word of caution here: human opinions are not welcomed during a Mastermind meeting and discussion of these spiritual principles. There is a difference between stating spiritual truths or relating a flash of inspiration and just giving your human opinion.

Spiritual truth comes through you but not from you. If you don't feel confident that what you're about to say is based on spiritual truth, save your comment for a simple conversation and not a Mastermind meeting.

On average you can expect your Mastermind meeting to last anywhere from one to two hours.

Am I ready to be committed to my Mastermind meetings?

_____

_____

_____

_____

_____

Chapter Fourteen

More About Forgiveness, Prayer, and the Law of Giving

Masterminding hinges on many spiritual principles. Forgiveness, prayer, and the Law of Giving are some of them.

More About Forgiveness

Jesus said, "And when you stand praying, if you hold anything against anyone, forgive him..." (Mark 11:25).

Again, in the Sermon on the Mount, Jesus said, "If you are offering your gift at the altar and there remember that your brother has something against you, leave your gift there in front of the altar. First, go and be reconciled to your brother, then come and offer your gift. Settle matters quickly with your adversary." (Matthew 5:23-25).

"Love your enemies and pray for those who persecute you..." (Matthew 5:44 and 45)

The Miracle Portal

"Do not judge, and you will not be judged. Do not condemn, and you will not be condemned. Forgive, and you will be forgiven." (Luke 6:37).

He also said, "Forgive us our debts as we also have forgiven our debtors…" (Matthew 6:12).

Jesus didn't say these things because he knew it would make a great 'sound byte' two thousand years later. He said them because they are spiritual laws people have to understand if they are to have happy and abundant lives. His point was that hanging onto unforgiveness weighs us down and chains us to the physical plane.

In the Mastermind Process, our goal is to rise above the physical plane to the spiritual plane, where the answers to our desires originate.

We don't forgive because terrible things were done to us but we're 'bigger' than all that. We forgive because if anything happened that was unlike good, it was unreal in the eternal sense. Holding a grudge over something unreal is as senseless as holding a grudge over a scene in a movie.

I'm sorry to say we haven't progressed very much since Jesus spoke his first words about forgiveness. Forgiveness is not a popular idea in our culture. Oh, we give lip service to it, because that's the 'right' thing to do, but how many of us truly practice forgiveness? Think about this. Are you practicing forgiveness? If not, you are delaying your good.

Does that mean the Mastermind won't help me with my desires if I don't forgive?

No. The Mastermind has already answered your desire in the invisible realm of Spirit. When you are in unforgiveness, you are blocking your desire.

How can you receive your desires from the Mastermind if you are wrapped up in the illusions of the world? You are not separate from another human being. Everyone is worthy of your forgiveness. We are all one with each other and one with the Creator.

We were all created by the Mastermind, and It created every single one of us good. Some of us may have behaved badly, made some wrong choices, and hurt people on the physical plane. But remember, the physical plane is a world of illusion.

It's playtime, dream time. If it wasn't good, it was never real in the eternal sense; the consequences are not eternal.

Murder is not eternal – there is no such thing as death. The spiritual realm is our real home and however we die we return home to spirit.

Stealing is not eternal – in the spiritual realm. In our spiritual home, we have everything we want.

Separation is not eternal. Every creation of the Mastermind in the entire universe, including every spiritual master, human being, animal, plant, rock, star, sun, alien, whatever, is one with each other, and with the Mastermind. We are all one in every way. *This is a lot to unpack. You may feel you need to read this section again.*

Even from the cross, Jesus said, "Father, forgive them, for they do not know what they are doing." (Luke 23:34).

That's true for every single person who has been hurtful toward us in any way. They did not know what they were doing, not in a spiritual sense. They will know when they reach the spiritual plane but by then they'll also understand none of it was real.

People always behave badly out of fear and ignorance. Fear and ignorance are abundant on the physical plane, but don't exist on the spiritual plane. We can choose to educate ourselves about the reality of spirit rather than be mesmerized by the physical plane.

We can choose to understand how the Mastermind's universe works and see through fear. The people or organizations involved in hurting us will remember these truths for themselves eventually, here or on the spiritual plane.

When we get to the spiritual plane we all remember the only thing that matters in hurtful human interactions is that we come away from them learning to love more. The same principle applies to every kind of hurt imaginable.

"A man's wisdom gives him patience; it is to his glory to overlook an offense." (Prov. 19:11).

Some Words About Prayer

Prayer is just another word for 'holding the vision.' Prayers are our thoughts and desires. Sometimes we consciously send them to the Mastermind, and sometimes we don't.

Whether we have intentional contact or not, the Universe knows every thought we think. The thoughts and feelings behind our desires are prayers.

When Jesus raised Lazarus from the dead, he prayed before he did so, saying, "Father, I thank you that you have heard me. I know that you always hear me…" (John 11:41-42).

The Mastermind always hears us. It knows everything we need even before we ask.

So when we pray, do we pray to inform the Mastermind of something It doesn't already know? Impossible. The Mastermind knows everything.

It knows the illusions under which we labor. It understands that our prayers almost always have to do with breaking through an Earthly illusion. It knows how real our needs feel. The Mastermind knows our needs.

Does the Mastermind want us to beg for something It knows we need?

Of course not! Our all-loving creator would not make Its children beg for their needs.

Jesus told us, "It is the Father's good pleasure to give you the Kingdom." (Luke 12:32). He didn't say, 'Beg and grovel and if you satisfy the Mastermind maybe you'll get your desire.'"

So why do we pray? Why do we seek conscious contact with the Mastermind if It hears our every thought, feeling, and desire anyway?

We pray so that we, on the physical plane, will feel closer to the Mastermind, not so that It will feel closer to us. We pray to remind *ourselves* – not the Mastermind – that It loves us, and will meet all our needs.

There's a little story that applies here. A husband and wife who had been married for over twenty-five years drove along with the husband at the wheel. They stopped at a long stop light and noticed a teenage couple in the car next to them. The girl was sitting as close as possible to her boyfriend who was in the driver's seat, and they were cuddling. In the other car, the wife said to her husband, "Aren't they cute? Don't you wish we still did things like that?" Her husband looked at her sitting at the opposite end of the front seat and said wryly, "I didn't go anywhere…"

The Miracle Portal

Just like the husband in the story, the Mastermind never retreated from us. It's the illusions of the physical plane that lead us to believe the lie of separation. We retreated from the Mastermind.

The Mastermind maintains us and constantly meets our every need, despite our ignorance of that fact. Every need or desire you ever had has been provided for you on the spiritual plane. If you haven't received it (yet) on the physical plane, it's because you didn't understand that, with the support of a like-minded group of others, you have to imagine it with feeling and faith, take action with a like-minded group of others, and draw it into physical manifestation.

Because prayer is thought and feeling, when we pray we need to strive to know that, even if we can't see it yet, the Mastermind is already helping us. We have to more than know it intellectually, we have to *feel* it emotionally. That's why so many spiritual teachers exhort us to give thanks before we see the results. Charles Fillmore said, "Thinking plus feeling equals a demonstration."

Certainly, we have reason to be excited when we pray. In the Sermon on the Mount, Jesus said, "Ask and it will be given to you; seek and you will find; knock and the door will be opened to you. For everyone who asks receives; he who seeks finds; and to him who knocks, the door will be opened. Which of you, if his son asks for bread, will give him a stone? Or if he asks for a fish, will give him a snake? If you know how to give good gifts to your children, how much more will your Father in heaven give good gifts to those who ask Him!" (Matthew 6:7-12).

In the New Thought movement, there is a system of prayer known as Denials and Affirmations. There are several wonderful books on the subject, and those are listed in the suggested readings at the end of this book.

Briefly, 'denial' means to deny the reality of evil or fear in any form. 'Affirmation' means to affirm the eternal spiritual presence of love which will bring the good into your experience.

You've probably already heard of affirming for your desires. It's becoming a popularly used tool today, though the technique is quite ancient.

One of the affirmation tools I use is called a vision book:

- Make a list of your desires.
- You have scrapbooked for your memories. Now scrapbook for your future. Cut out and paste pictures and words that positively illustrate your desire. If your desire is a dream house, find pictures of your dream house. Headline that page, 'My Dream Home,' or 'I Deserve to Own my Home.' Do this for each desire and use as many pages as you like.
- Place affirmations by the pictures. Next to your dream home you might write, 'I'm grateful to have my new house at a price and financing I can comfortably afford,' and 'The Mastermind meets all my desires.'
- Place all the pictures together in a notebook and look at them as frequently as you can.
- Spend time imagining yourself receiving your desires. Imagine them so clearly and strongly that you evoke the same feelings you would have if the desires manifested right now.

- Take positive action in faith toward your goal. Start looking at houses!

- As each desire is met, take those pictures out and add new pictures. Do you need to furnish your new house?

- Create a Gratitude Book with the pictures of desires you have already demonstrated. Look at it frequently with gratitude and acknowledgment of the power of the Mastermind.

In ending this segment on prayer, let me quote what Paul said, it's still good advice today. "Finally, brothers, whatever is true, whatever is noble, whatever is right, whatever is pure, whatever is lovely, whatever is admirable – if anything is excellent or praiseworthy – think about such things." (Phil. 3:4).

The Law of Giving

This is taught by every spiritual belief system around the world. Giving is a spiritual law. It is the secret of permanent prosperity. Giving creates a vacuum that enables you to receive.

This is Spiritual Law? In what way?

The Spiritual laws in the Bible are written in the quaint language of Biblical times. Today we quote laws this way: 'For every action, there is an equal and opposite reaction.' If we were to quote the Law of Giving in today's language, we might say, 'If you wish to receive, you must honor the flow of energy and give.'

Many religious sects speak to their members about tithing, giving ten percent of everything they receive to the religious community. If that's where you think your gift will be most appropriate, do that.

If, on the other hand, you are moved to give to a charity, to the needy, to a relief fund, or to a relative or friend who has a special need, do that. The point is you need to acknowledge you are an instrument used by the Mastermind to bring good to Its children.

I don't believe there's a set amount that 'should' be given. If you can't give a tenth, give a hundredth; or if you have it to give, make it fifty percent; whatever you're led to do by the Mastermind.

Nancy Reynolds

I'm reminded of the story of the poor widow in the Gospel of Luke. She was looked down upon by the powerful in the Synagogue because she had little to give as a tithe. She gave two mites, which was the smallest Roman coin made, the equivalent to the American penny. But Jesus said, "...this poor widow has put in more than all of them; for they gave out of their abundance and surplus; but she has contributed out of her lack and want..."

If you don't have money to give, then give something else: food, clothing, blankets, shoes, books, or volunteer time. If you have little to give at this moment, give what you can with a sincere intention to give good to another, and the Mastermind will provide the increase.

The Mastermind is the source of all our good, including money. Giving is an acknowledgment that you understand the Mastermind to be your source.

Jesus, understanding the law of giving and receiving, told us, "Give and gifts will be given to you... For with the measure you deal out, it will be measured back to you." (Luke 6:38).

The Miracle Portal

Do you believe you are one with everyone and everything in the universe?

_____
_____
_____
_____

Do you believe the Mastermind is furnishing your desires before you ask?

_____
_____
_____
_____

In what way are you fulfilling the law of giving? (Time, talent, things, or money?)

_____
_____
_____
_____
_____
_____

CHAPTER FIFTEEN
More Demonstrations

I want to end this book about the Mastermind Process by looking at more demonstrations reported by the Mastermind group members I've interviewed.

Carol, one of my Mastermind partners, desperately needed a new car, and we had been Masterminding about it for several weeks. First, she was led to investigate her credit report, where she found several incorrect items. She'd initially been afraid of the process of correcting her credit, but found with the Mastermind's help she could do it fairly quickly.

Next, she shopped around at several different new car lots, but each wanted too much money down or didn't have the right payment plan; something was wrong with every deal.

Meanwhile, she spent a fortune on her old car, trying her best to maintain it. Finally, her car completely quit running one day, and she had to leave it at a shopping center and walk home.

Carol was discouraged and exasperated, but she was also absolutely convinced the Mastermind would help her. Still, she had no car and no way to buy a new one. She held to the truth that the Mastermind provided her transportation, just as it provided for all her other needs.

Within one week all the money she needed for a down payment showed up as gifts – one a large amount of money from a person she barely knew. She found a brand-new car that had the payment plan she wanted and could afford.

Within one week a woman who was stranded in a parking lot with no money had a brand new car! I never asked what happened to the old car. I wonder if it's still in that parking lot?

Christy, another of my Mastermind partners, experienced some uncomfortable conflicts with a new management team at her company. She tried for six months to work out these conflicts through the chain of command and nothing resolved the situation.

Christy took her need for resolution of her work problems to her Mastermind group. We visioned together for the resolution of the conflict "for the highest good of all concerned."

After a few weeks of Masterminding on this issue, Christy was led to submit her resignation with two weeks' notice, though she had no other job in the offing. That evening she went to a class for a university program she had been enrolled in for some time. During a break, she shared with another student about needing another job. While she was speaking, a second student who was the manager of a rival company overheard her conversation, interrupted, and offered her a new job there and then. It didn't take long for the Mastermind to work the situation out for Christy's highest good. She's very happy at her new job, and the company is delighted to have such a pleasant and positive employee.

Greg from Las Vegas had a trailer to sell. It was important that the trailer be sold quickly because costly payments were due, though he was no longer using it. Greg tried for some months, unsuccessfully, to sell the trailer before taking his need to his Mastermind group. After the Mastermind meeting, a prospective buyer called to look at the trailer. He looked at it, liked it, and wrote out a check for the entire amount.

Greg also tells about a time when his ex-wife went to court demanding higher child support. Greg was quite willing to support his children, he just didn't know where he was going to get the money to meet the increased child support demands.

He took his need to his Mastermind group. The next day Greg's boss talked to him at work. The company was extremely pleased with his performance and felt he deserved a raise. Greg received a raise that was effective immediately and more than covered his increased child support payments.

Kitty from Las Vegas talked about her loneliness after her divorce. She wanted a new relationship with a wonderful man, though she didn't know anyone who fit the bill. She took the desire to her Mastermind group and three months later she met a wonderful man and fell in love. Now they're engaged.

Kitty also tells a story about how she wanted to resume playing the clarinet. She had played professionally at one time, but had given it up and sold her instrument. She felt it was time to get into her music again, but she no longer had the clarinet. A new one would cost at least $1000.00 – money she didn't have. Kitty took her desire to her Mastermind group. About three months later, a woman she barely knew approached her. The woman explained she'd heard through a mutual friend of Kitty's desire to begin playing the clarinet again. The woman explained her husband, who had passed away, had been a professional clarinet player, and she would love to see his beloved instrument put to work again. She gave the clarinet to Kitty, along with all her husband's other equipment, a gift that far exceeded the $1000.00 Kitty had estimated. Best of all, the woman adamantly refused to accept payment for any of it.

Dee from San Diego tells about Masterminding for her daughter's wedding. It was a huge and costly wedding. Like many such weddings, there were a million details to work out, including the use of a yacht. At the last minute, they were forced to accept many substitutions in their original plans. However, Dee knew she had Masterminded about the situation, and she trusted the Mastermind to work everything to perfection. That's just how everything worked out. The wedding was a huge success, and Dee's daughter told her before she left on her honeymoon, "You created heaven on Earth for that four hours."

All these stories are not flukes. The information contained in this book is time-tested and proven.

Just as the principles of Mathematics work every time so does the Mastermind process.

Stop living a life of quiet desperation. The Mastermind is waiting, longing for you to ask for Its help. Ask today.

I can't wait to hear about your miracles.

Are you willing to receive from the Mastermind in unexpected ways?

_____

_____

_____

Nancy Reynolds

_____
_____
_____
_____
_____
_____
_____
_____

ALTHOUGH THIS IS
THE END OF THE BOOK,
THIS IS THE BEGINNING
OF YOUR ADVENTURE
WITH MASTERMINDING.
*THIS IS YOUR LAUNCH,
THE NEXT STAGE FOR YOU IS UP!*

SUGGESTED AUTHORS

Listed below are some of the wonderful spiritual teachers who have influenced my life and informed this work.

We have so many opportunities to read, see and hear these wonderful teachers. Most of these people have multiple works. Let your intuition lead you to the format that suits you best.

- Abraham-Hicks, Abraham-Hicks Publications - Law of Attraction Official Site, https://www.abraham-hicks.com
- Rev. Jack Boland
- Dr. H. Emilie Cady
- Kryon Channeled by Lee Carroll
- Deepak Chopra, M.D.
- Mary Baker Eddy, Christian Science Church
- Emmet Fox
- Edwene Gaines,
- https://edwenegaines.wwwhubs.com/
- Louise Hay, https://www.louisehay.com/
- Napoleon Hill
- Emma Curtis Hopkins
- Cash Peters
- Catherine Ponder
- Helen Schucman
- Paul Selig

Bibliography

Boland, Jack, "The Master Mind Principle." Warren, Michigan,: Master Mind Publishing Company. 1983.

Cady, H. Emilie, <u>Lessons In Truth</u>. Unity Village, Mo,: Unity Books. 1995.

Eddy, Mary Baker, <u>Science and Health With Key to the Scriptures</u>. Boston, Massachusetts: The First Church of Christ, Scientist. 1991.

Fillmore, Charles, and Cora, <u>Teach Us To Pray</u>. Unity Village, Mo,: Unity School of Christianity. 1941.

Gaines, Edwene, "Prosperity Plus," Mentone, Al.: Prosperity Products. 1985.

Hill, Napolean, <u>Think and Grow Rich</u>, Hollywood, Florida.: Lifetime Books, 1998.

Lazaris, "Lazaris Interviews." Beverly Hills, Ca.: Concept Synergy Publishing. 1988.

John Milton's "Paradise Lost." Edited and with an Introduction by Harold Bloom. New York: Chelsea House. 1996.

Schumann, Helen, and Thetford, William, *A Course in Miracles*. Glen Ellen, Ca.: Foundation for Inner Peace. 1992.

Schwarz, Cindy, *A Tour of the Subatomic Zoo: A Guide to Particle Physics*. Woodbury, N.Y.: American Institute of Physics. 1997.

Zondervan (Author), *Amplified Holy Bible*. Zondervan Publishing. 2017.

BIOGRAPHY

Nancy has been a Registered Nurse for forty years, over half of which has been in hospice care. She received her Doctor of Philosophy in Transpersonal Psychology in 2002 but chose to continue working as a nurse with hospice patients.

This year finds her semi-retired in a plains state where she writes and teaches about the Mastermind Process.

Nancy works with spiritual seekers who wish to improve their relationships with reality. She encourages them to release fear in favor of the knowledge that we live as creators in a world designed for our growth.

The Mastermind Process teaches all who practice it to abandon limitations and rely on the superior knowledge of a Higher Power. As a result, they experience inspiration that helps them manifest their greatest desires.

www.ingramcontent.com/pod-product-compliance
Lightning Source LLC
Chambersburg PA
CBHW020534080526
44583CB00013B/856